USA TODAY

Lifeline

BIOGRAPHIES

VERA WANG
Enduring Style

by Katherine Krohn

Twenty-First Century Books · Minneapolis

FOR BABY AND STARCHY, MY FOREVER FRIENDS

Twenty-First Century Books
A division of Lerner Publishing Group, Inc.
241 First Avenue North
Minneapolis, MN 55401 U.S.A.

Website address: www.lernerbooks.com

The publisher wishes to thank Richard Curtis, Susan Weiss, and Ben Nussbaum of USA TODAY for their help in preparing this book.

Library of Congress Cataloging-in-Publication Data

Vera Wang : enduring style / by Katherine Krohn.
        p.   cm. — (Lifeline biographies)
    Includes bibliographical references and index.
    ISBN 978–1–58013–572–6 (lib. bdg. : alk. paper)
    1. Wang, Vera—Juvenile literature. 2. Wang, Vera. 3. Women fashion designers—New York (State)—New York—Biography—Juvenile literature. 4. Women fashion designers—New York (State)—New York—Biography. I. Title.
TT505.W36T63 2009
746.9'2092—dc22   2008009198 [B]

Manufactured in the United States of America
1 2 3 4 5 6 – PA – 14 13 12 11 10 09

USA TODAY Lifeline BIOGRAPHIES

Too frilly: In 1989, when Vera Wang was planning her wedding, she found most bridal shops offered frilly, girlish dresses. This style reminded Wang of the female figure that often sits on top of a wedding cake. At nearly forty years old, she thought the style was too young and silly for her. She ended up designing her own wedding dress.

A Modern Woman

In 1989 thirty-nine-year-old Vera Wang was a high-powered, high-fashion design director. She was also engaged to marry businessman Arthur Becker, and she wanted the perfect dress for her wedding day. But even though she visited stores all over New York City, she found only traditional, fussy gowns, designed for a younger bride. "I'm very modern and sophisticated," Wang said. "I didn't want to look like the girl on top of the wedding cake."

Frustrated at the lack of options, Wang decided that she would simply have to create her own dress. Fortunately, with more than fifteen years of experience in the fashion industry, Wang knew a thing or two about style and design. Wang hired a seamstress to sew her design, a hand-beaded white gown with a full skirt. "No one was doing dresses that addressed the modern woman," said Wang. "I wanted something more sleek and minimal."

Soon after her wedding, Wang made an important decision. She knew there was a need for more sophisticated, elegant wedding gowns. Six months after her wedding, Wang quit her job as a design director for fashion designer Ralph Lauren. She opened a two-story boutique (a small shop that sells expensive or unique clothing and accessories) in the upscale Carlyle Hotel in New York City.

At first, Wang sold wedding gowns by designers she admired, such as Carolina Herrera and Christian Dior. Within months, she was selling her own, unique haute couture (made-to-order, one-of-a-kind) designs. Word of Wang's designs spread quickly among well-to-do New Englanders, upper-class

First shop: Wang's first bridal shop was located in the Carlyle Hotel on East 76th Street, not far from New York City's main shopping district.

socialites, and celebrities. Vera Wang soon became the foremost designer of wedding gowns in the world.

But Wang's story doesn't stop at bridal dresses. She has also designed one-of-a-kind formal gowns for many top celebrities. Oprah Winfrey, Whoopi Goldberg, and Hillary Rodham Clinton all love Wang's designs. Actresses Rachel Weisz, Helen Hunt, Sharon Stone, Keira Knightley, Cate Blanchett, Alicia Silverstone, and Halle Berry are all devoted customers of Wang's. Celebrities don her gowns for award ceremonies, movie

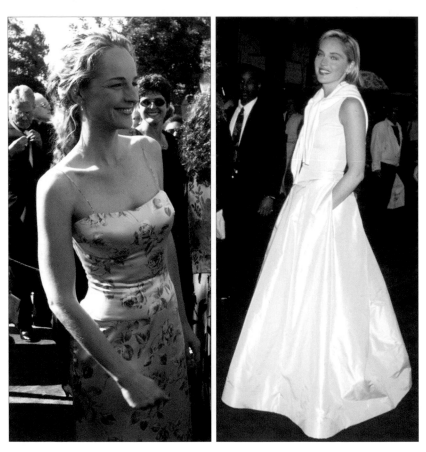

Cool customers: When actresses gather for major award ceremonies, many wear designs by Vera Wang. Helen Hunt *(left)* and Sharon Stone *(right)* appeared in Wang gowns in the mid-1990s.

premieres, and other important events. "Vera's designs are very simple but not boring," said actress Holly Hunter, a friend of Wang's. Wang is known for simply constructed, slinky gowns that drape smoothly over a woman's body.

Wang's evening wear and sportswear collections are also popular, as is her ready-to-wear clothing (designs sold in finished condition and in standard sizes, rather than made to order). She designs personal and household items as well. These products range from champagne glasses, fine stationery, and fragrance, to candles, bedding, and collectible Barbie dolls. Her products are sold in upscale department stores such as Saks Fifth Avenue, Neiman Marcus, and Barneys New York. She has opened two Vera Wang boutiques in New York City, as well as boutiques in Canada, China, and Europe.

Yet, despite her huge success, Wang has had no formal training as a designer. Instead, she has a natural talent. Her skill and eye for design had been cultivated by attending fashion shows in Paris as a child. She spent years studying art history and worked as a fashion editor at *Vogue* magazine for sixteen years.

When Vera Wang opened her first store in 1990, she didn't even know if she would last a year. Nearly twenty years later, she is the owner and CEO of a multimillion-dollar business. From a frustrated bride-to-be with a passion for clothing and design, she has become one of the superstars of international fashion.

Park Avenue: After achieving business success, Vera's father—Cheng Ching Wang—set up his family in a large apartment on Park Avenue. This famous boulevard in New York City is known for its high real estate prices and prime location on the Upper East Side of Manhattan (one of New York's administrative divisions).

Finding Her Fashion Sense

Vera Ellen Wang was born on June 27, 1949, in New York City. Baby Vera had delicate, pretty features and glossy black hair. The Wang family lived in a big apartment on Park Avenue in New York City. The house had fine furniture, antique fixtures, and original paintings by Renoir and Monet on the walls.

The Wangs lived in a fourteen-room duplex apartment at 740 Park Avenue, an exclusive address in Manhattan. Vera's father purchased the apartment in 1983 for $350,000 (about $600,000 in modern money). After her father's death in 2006, Vera bought the apartment from the Cheng Ching Wang estate for $23 million.

Vera's parents came from wealthy and influential families in China. Her father, Cheng Ching Wang, was born in Shanghai, China. His own father had been the war minister under Chiang Kai-shek, a major military and political leader in China from the 1920s through the 1940s. Vera's mother, Florence Wu, was the daughter of a warlord (a powerful military leader).

Cheng and Florence were married in 1939. In the mid-1940s, they left China and moved to the United States. Like many Chinese immigrants to the United States at the time, they were fleeing China's Communist Revolution. Taking place in the first half of the twentieth century, the revolution was a violent time in Chinese history. During the revolution,

Chinese leader: Vera's grandfather worked for Chinese leader Chiang Kai-shek (*above*).

Leaving turmoil: People in Shanghai, China, fight to buy rice in the 1940s, around the time Vera's parents left China. During that period, China had just survived World War II (1939–1945) but was still fighting a civil war.

the Communist Party of China overthrew the existing government and formed the People's Republic of China. Civil war wracked the country, forcing Vera's parents and thousands of other people to leave China and seek a safer and more peaceful life elsewhere.

After settling in the United States, Vera's father established a company that made medicinal drugs. The company thrived, doing business in both the United States and in Asia. Vera's mother worked as a translator for the United Nations, an international organization with its headquarters in New York City. The Wangs soon started their family. Two years after the birth

Name recognition: Vera's name as it is written in Chinese characters

of baby Vera, Vera's brother, Kenneth, was born. "They fully embraced the American philosophy," Vera said later about her parents. Their motto was "'This is the land of opportunity. Let's go for it.'"

A Love of Fashion

Florence Wang was elegant, poised, and self-confident. She loved fashion and style. Young Vera admired the designer clothing in her mother's closet and the stylish way she dressed. At an early age, Vera learned an appreciation for fine things, beauty, and design. She could see how a simple piece of clothing or a flashy accessory—such as a bangle bracelet or a colorful hat or high-heeled shoes—could transform the way a person looked. "I grew up loving fashion," says Wang.

Learning from Mom: Magazine writers scribble notes at a Christian Dior fashion show in Paris in the 1950s. Vera's mother, Florence Wang, instilled in her daughter a strong sense of high fashion. Mother and daughter went to fashion shows in Paris. They were especially fond of the designs of Yves Saint Laurent, who was working for the Dior house at the time.

During her childhood in the 1950s and 1960s, Vera's mother took her to fashion shows in Paris. Young Vera learned to love the sophisticated clothing made by top designers such as Hubert de Givenchy and Christian Dior.

Vera's mother also took her along on shopping trips, during which her mother purchased expensive, made-to-order designs to fill her closets. One of Vera's mother's favorite stores was Yves Saint Laurent's shop in Paris. From an early age, Vera admired Laurent's chic, creative designs. "We were one of Saint Laurent's best clients," remembers Vera.

World Traveler

Vera attended the Chapin School, an exclusive, all-girls school on the island of Manhattan. (Manhattan is one of the five main divisions, called boroughs, of New York City.) The school focused on both academic achievement and creativity. Vera grew to love the arts in many forms—painting, design, architecture, and drama.

Junior year: Vera posed for a picture at the Chapin School in 1966, her junior year.

While Vera received a world-class education at Chapin, she also traveled worldwide with her family. Instead of flying, the Wang family traveled by ship, taking ocean liners such as the *Mauretania* or the *Queen Mary*. "What a fantasy-land—I had free run of the ship," Vera recalled later. "Back then travel wasn't about speed, it was about the process."

Travel was fun for Vera and her brother, and it also helped

Traveling by Ship

Built in the 1930s, both the *Maure-tania* and the *Queen Mary* became troop transport ships during World War II. After the war, they were converted into cruise ships. By the mid-1960s, as the popularity of air travel grew, both ships were retired. A Scottish shipping company bought the *Mauretania* for scrap metal. The city of Long Beach, California, purchased the *Queen Mary*, making it a unique museum, hotel, and conference center.

Shipboard adventures: With New York's skyline in the background, the luxury liner *Queen Mary* steams out of New York Harbor,

them learn about different cultures. Their worldly parents helped too. Vera's parents spoke both English and Mandarin (a form of the Chinese language). Vera also learned to speak Mandarin, along with other languages such as French.

Passion for Skating

Vera's parents expected their children to do well in school. Vera was a good student, but she also enjoyed physical activities. One of her early loves was ballet, which she began studying at about the age of eight. Vera even attended the world-renowned School of American Ballet in New York City.

But an even greater passion for Vera would turn out to be figure skating. She had first gotten a taste of the sport when she was seven years old. That year her parents had given her a pair of ice skates. They signed her up for skating lessons, and by 1959, at the age of ten, Vera was serious about skating.

Even as a child, Vera had a great deal of self-discipline. And she knew that she would have to work very hard if she wanted to compete at the top levels of figure skating. She dreamed of one day being good enough to take part in the figure-skating competition of the Olympic Games. Pushing herself to be better and better, she got up every morning at six o'clock to practice skating before school. "She was very willing to work hard. She had a passion and a hunger for skating," said Vera's coach, Sonya Dunfield.

In the late 1960s, Vera teamed with a talented male skater she knew named James Stuart. Vera and James competed together in the 1968 and 1969 U.S. Figure Skating Championships, winning fifth place in 1969. But after the competition, Stuart decided to skate solo. Vera wasn't sure what she wanted to do. She loved to skate, but she also had other dreams. She had begun to consider going to medical school. Should she take a gamble and dedicate all of her time to skating? She knew that doing so would mean long hours of training with little time left for anything else. Or should she pursue a career as a doctor instead?

College Girl

Nineteen-year-old Vera decided that she would not abandon skating completely. She would, however, enter college and see where that path might take her. So she enrolled at Sarah Lawrence College, a private school located just north of New York City. Vera took the typical classes of a premed (premedical school) student, such as chemistry, anatomy, and physiology. While she was an excellent student, she still found the classes to be demanding. And she soon realized that she had little time to practice skating. At that point, Vera made a very difficult decision. With hesitation and sadness, she gave up her dream of being a competitive figure skater.

Vera felt lost without skating and overwhelmed by her difficult, premed classes. She wasn't sure if she really wanted to be a doctor. During her sophomore year of college, Vera dropped out of school. Shocking her parents, she moved to Paris and started a relationship with a young man she had met four years earlier, French Olympic skater Patrick Pera. Pera was well known in Paris at the time—especially after he won a bronze medal at the 1968 Winter Olympics. Photographers from the press photographed Vera and Patrick together. The couple was even featured on the cover of the magazine *Paris Match*.

Skating romance: In the late 1960s, Vera became involved with Patrick Pera, a skilled French figure skater who took the bronze medal at the 1968 Winter Olympics. Vera herself had had a short figure-skating career.

Paris Match is a weekly French magazine that focuses on the activities of celebrities. In the early 1970s, when Vera was in Paris, it also covered the Vietnam War (1957–1975) and French student protests.

Vera enrolled at the University of Paris–Sorbonne. The architecture, fashion, and design of Paris inspired her and reawakened her lifelong love of art. Vera took classes in art history and studied foreign languages during her years in Paris.

The Sorbonne: Part of the University of Paris, the Sorbonne was built in the seventeenth century. Vera attended the Sorbonne in the late 1970s.

Return to New York

Vera's relationship with Patrick Pera didn't work out. In 1970 twenty-one-year-old Vera moved back to New York City. About one year later, Vera returned to Sarah Lawrence to complete her college education. Vera's time in Paris had helped her make an important decision. She had realized that she did not truly want to become a doctor. Medicine could be a great career, but it was not where her heart lay. Instead, she decided, she would pursue a degree in art history.

While Vera was a student at Sarah Lawrence, she got the chance to live abroad during her junior and senior years. Vera chose to go back to Paris, a city she still loved very much. She liked the art museums, sidewalk cafés, and architecture of the great French capital. And she adored the cutting-edge fashion for which Paris is famous. In her early twenties, Vera was getting a clearer idea of what she wanted to do with her life.

 Other Sarah Lawrence alumni include journalist Barbara Walters, actress Joanne Woodward, and artist Yoko Ono.

"When you're in Paris, you can't help but notice fashion. I wanted something to do with fashion," Vera recalls. "I would have done anything. I would have swept floors. I would have licked envelopes. I just wanted to be a part of it."

Sense of style: In 1968 Vera showed off her sense of style during her debut at the International Debutante Ball in New York. This event marks the entrance into society of a young woman, usually from an upper-class family. The debutantes typically wear fancy white gowns. Later in her life, Vera would design gowns for debutantes around the country.

Days and Nights at Vogue

■■■■

During Vera's summer break from Sarah Lawrence, she returned home to New York City. She landed a job as a salesgirl at the exclusive Yves Saint Laurent boutique located on Manhattan's Madison Avenue. The surrounding neighborhood is filled with department stores, fashionable shops, advertising agencies, and luxurious hotels. Vera loved being in this bustling part of New York. Even more, she loved being surrounded by the creations of a designer whom she had admired her whole life.

IN FOCUS

Yves Saint Laurent

Born in 1936, Yves Saint Laurent slipped into the French fashion industry with the help of famed designer Christian Dior. With Dior's death in 1957, young Saint Laurent took over the Dior house. By 1962 Saint Laurent had started his own haute couture house and had shown his first collection.

Saint Laurent spearheaded many fashion statements that are now taken for granted. He integrated ethnic themes from Africa and Asia and glamorized male-inspired attire, such as the classic tuxedo suit, for women. Throughout the 1960s, Vera and her mother shopped at Saint Laurent's salon. His Rive Gauche boutique opened in Paris in 1966. Its high-end but ready-to-wear clothing was Saint Laurent's attempt to bring fashion into everyday life. He was also the first to use black models in his fashion shows. Retired since 2002, Saint Laurent spends much of his time at his home in Marrakech, Morocco.

Rive Gauche: In the mid-1960s, designer Yves Saint Laurent stood outside his Paris boutique called Rive Gauche. In front of him, a model wears a skirt and sweater from his ready-to-wear collection.

First Fashion Job

Vera already knew that she loved clothes, and she liked working with them. She had fond memories of accompanying her fashion-loving mother on shopping trips and dress fittings in New York City and Paris. But she also found that she enjoyed working with the customers who came to Laurent's shop looking for beautiful clothing. In the process of watching her mother select and try on clothing, Vera had developed a special talent for helping women dress well. Vera's knowledge of art helped her as well. She had a great ability to see which clothing worked on a woman's body frame and which clothing did not. She also had a flair for pairing the right color of dress with a woman's skin tone and hair color.

Vera found that her job had other perks too. She had the opportunity to meet important people in the fashion industry. One regular customer of the store, Frances Patiky Stein, was an editor at *Vogue*, the international fashion magazine. Stein liked Vera right away. She admired Vera's high energy, enthusiasm, and intelligence. She could also tell that Vera really loved clothes and had a special style of her own. Stein had a hunch that Vera also had a special eye for fashion—that special something that would make her fit in well at *Vogue*. Vera was surprised when Stein asked her to give her a call after she graduated from college. Maybe she could find a job for Vera at *Vogue*, she said. Vera was flattered. *Vogue* was a highly celebrated publication. She told Stein that she would give the offer serious thought.

After completing her college studies, Vera wasn't exactly sure what to do with her life. Her ambitions were high and wide ranging, but they had become more and more focused on the arts. She dreamed of becoming an actress, for example. But she also thought about enrolling in fashion school. She loved fashion and felt that she could design clothing. In fashion school, Vera reasoned, she could learn the business of the fashion industry and find out what it takes to become a designer. Vera decided to talk to her father about her idea. Like many Chinese Americans, Vera was raised to honor her parents. And honoring her parents meant sharing with them any major decisions that she made in her life.

"I want to be a designer," Vera told her father. She explained that she felt fashion school would be a way for her to get started in the fashion industry. Vera's father thought for a moment. His mood was serious. He replied, "What makes you think you can be a designer? I want to see you get a job in fashion first."

Vera was disappointed. But then she began to wonder if her father might be right. Maybe she did need to work inside the fashion industry. That way she could see if being a fashion designer was something she really wanted to pursue. After all, she had many passions. How did she know this was the most important one?

Then Vera remembered *Vogue* editor Frances Patiky Stein's invitation to give her a call when she was done with college. At first Vera wasn't sure if she really wanted to work at *Vogue*. Creating and designing interested her much more than an office job at a magazine. But she realized that working at *Vogue* would "incorporate all of the things she loved," such as clothing, style, fashion, art, and design.

Vera decided that a job at *Vogue* was something she couldn't pass up. So she gave Stein a call. She was thrilled when Stein offered her a job as an editorial assistant. Vera planned to work at the magazine for a year or two, until she figured out what she wanted to do next.

***Vogue* opportunity:** Frances Patiky Stein (*above*) offered Wang a job at *Vogue* after seeing her potential at Yves Saint Laurent.

Vogue: Influencing Fashion

Founded in 1892, *Vogue* has become synonymous with high fashion and high society. The magazine also publishes articles on other topics, such as art and politics. Condé Nast, *Vogue*'s parent company, has started spinoffs of the original magazine—including *Men's Vogue*, *Teen Vogue*, and *Vogue Living*. Different editions of *Vogue* are published around the world, including in Australia, Brazil, China, Japan, Mexico, Britain, and India.

Supermodels—including Twiggy, Cindy Crawford, Gia Carangi, Kate Moss, and Gisele Bundchen—have appeared on *Vogue*'s covers over the years. They have become international celebrities. Its editors in chief, all women, have put their stamp on generations of the fashion industry.

Current editor in chief Anna Wintour took over in 1988. Since then she has become a much-admired and much-criticized icon. Wintour's ex-assistant wrote the successful novel *The Devil Wears Prada*, about a

Cover shot: A *Vogue* cover from the 1970s

fictional fashion magazine and its bitter editor in chief. Nevertheless, the novel and later movie reiterated the power that glamour magazines like *Vogue* have on the fashion industry.

New Kid on the Block

For her first day of work, Wang was eager to impress her boss. She looked through her closet and tried on outfit after outfit. Finally, she decided on one of her favorite dresses, a stylish Yves Saint Laurent creation. She had recently purchased the dress on a trip to Paris with her mother. Wang painted her fingernails black—a trend that was popular in Paris at the time. Vera's new boss didn't care for Vera's polished, glamorous appearance. "Go home and get changed, because you're going to be doing dirt work," she ordered. Vera felt embarrassed. But she did what her supervisor said. She went home and changed into a casual pair of jeans.

Vogue, a magazine known for cutting-edge fashion trends and excellent photography, moved and inspired Vera. "*Vogue* is the best training ground any young woman could have," Vera later said.

Vera soon learned that working at *Vogue* as an assistant didn't mean sitting at a desk all day. And there was little time for lunch or coffee breaks. But Vera didn't mind. She helped with whatever needed doing. She did general office work, ran errands, photocopied papers, and hauled heavy equipment for photo shoots. Vera was a hard worker. She was full of positive, creative energy and enthusiasm. Her bosses were impressed by her dedication. "Vera had all the ingredients of a star," one of Vera's first bosses at *Vogue*, Polly Allen Mellen, later said. Very soon Vera had risen to be a fashion editor—making her the youngest in *Vogue* history.

Learning the ropes: Polly Allen Mellen tutored Vera in her early days at *Vogue*.

The Right Eye

In addition to her energy, Vera had an eye for fashion, style, and design. "Eye is a new way of viewing something old," Vera explained. "Everything's been done in fashion. It's how you bring newness to the concept. I mean, a white shirt is a white shirt, but how do you wear it?"

Photo shoots: Supermodel Gia Carangi poses during a *Vogue* photo shoot. As Vera got more experience, she came to be in charge of these sessions. She visualized how the model would be posed and how her clothes would look. She had input on makeup and props—anything that would make a photo look fresh and new.

At *Vogue*, part of Vera's job was to look for new ways to see something old. One of her duties was setting up photo shoots. She thought about what should be in the picture, how the models should stand, how they should wear the clothes, and what their makeup should look like. Her job was to help make each piece of clothing look as fresh, new, and exciting as possible. "Those are the things that editors are always searching for, particularly in a picture because you only have so long to capture the magic of fashions," Vera pointed out.

Working at *Vogue* opened Vera's eyes to a bigger, even more fascinating world of fashion. One of the valuable experiences that the magazine gave her was close contact with designers, which helped her better understand the fashion business. For example, she formed friendships with top designers, such as Calvin Klein and Ralph Lauren. She gained insight into how designers become successful in the business, how they come up with new designs, and how they take an idea and turn it into an actual piece of clothing.

Climbing the Ladder

In 1973, at the age of twenty-five, Vera Wang had been promoted to the position of senior fashion editor at *Vogue*. She worked long hours at her job. She didn't

Getting insight: Designer Calvin Klein *(above)* helped Vera gain experience in the fashion industry in the 1980s.

as if like she had time for a serious personal life. Many nights, Vera worked late into the night at her job. "I lived at *Vogue*," she said.

Before long, she was promoted again. This time she became a European editor for American *Vogue* in Paris. In her new job, Vera was expected to socialize with powerful, glamorous people, such as supermodels and internationally famous designers. Vera came from a wealthy family and a privileged background, and she had met many prominent and high-powered people. But she didn't like her new duties. Working at *Vogue*'s Paris office "was a little grand for me as a job. I like the gritty parts of fashion, the design, the studio, the pictures," said Vera. "I'm not really a girl who likes to go out to lunch or cocktails or store openings. I felt very removed. It wasn't just that I didn't like having lunch with Gianni Versace, it was just that I wanted to be a designer still. Very much."

Disco Nights

Even after her long workdays at *Vogue*, Vera was rarely ready to go home and rest. Instead, she often headed out for an evening of fun and partying with friends. And New York City offered a rich and exciting nightlife. It was "a wild, wild period of fashion and music," Vera later said.

Vera especially loved going to the nightclub Studio 54. In the 1970s and 1980s, Studio 54 was the hottest place to be in New York City. The exclusive club was packed with artists, musicians, and celebrities who were dancing, chatting, and hanging out. On some nights, Vera would socialize and dance at Studio 54 until the early morning hours. Then, instead of going home, she would take a taxi right back to work.

Party on: Dozens of people crowded the dance floor at Studio 54 in the early 1980s.

And so, before long, Vera returned to New York City and the job she loved. But she continued to hold tightly to her dream of one day being a designer herself.

Career Woman

In 1980, when Vera was thirty-one years old, she met Arthur Becker at a tennis tournament. Becker—a successful stockbroker and business-man—was handsome, funny, and friendly. He liked Vera immediately, and he asked her out on a date. But Vera turned down his offer. Becker was disappointed. Vera simply explained that she didn't want to date anyone at that point in her life. She wasn't ready for a relationship. "At that point I was like, 'No way! I have a career, I have places to go, people to see,'" Vera later said.

Throughout her twenties and into her thirties, Vera poured her energy and passion into her job at *Vogue*. When she first started working for the magazine, she had intended to stay for only a year or two. She had expected to get bored eventually and move on to something else. Her job at *Vogue*, however, proved to be the education of a lifetime. Vera learned the fashion business from the inside out—a firsthand education that a degree in fashion design wouldn't have given her. "*Vogue* is a seductive place because of what you get to see and what you're privy to; it's a world that I can't even explain," Vera said.

Moving on: Designer Geoffrey Beene examines shoes at a shop in Milan, Italy. He was known for his strict attention to detail, a trait Wang much admired. So when Beene offered her a job, she was thrilled.

Finally Designing

Working at *Vogue* was a challenging and thrilling experience for Wang. It also opened the door for future opportunities. While working for the magazine, Wang met and interacted with many top designers. One of them, Geoffrey Beene, offered her a job. Wang decided that she would take the position. She loved how Beene paid so much attention to detail. "Geoffrey was a real artist," said Wang, "and he wanted people around who would be fretting over a collar for a long time. That's what I loved."

www.usatoday.com

USA TODAY

Life

SECTION D

February 9, 1988

The best of Geoffrey Beene

From the Pages of
USA TODAY

A bespectacled, white-haired Southern gentleman from Haynesville, La., [Geoffrey] Beene, 60, is widely considered the USA's greatest designer. His sumptuous, custom fabrics and extravagant attention to detail elevate ready to-wear to the level of haute couture—at close-to-couture prices of $1,200 to $15,000 a pop.

Beene's supreme strength is his knack for creating timeless fashions rather than jumping on the trend of the moment. "It's sort of a challenge I've always made to myself," says the soft-spoken designer. "I try to make clothes that are very contemporary and modern without being bizarre. I hate clothes that look dated."

"You could put his dresses from the '60s in somebody's line again and you would not know which year they were from," says June Weir, executive fashion editor of *Harper's Bazaar*. "He's in the same league as Yves Saint Laurent."

—Elizabeth Sporkin, February 9, 1988

But as it turned out, Beene was not the only designer who admired Wang's talent. In fact, the very same day that she was supposed to begin working for Beene, she received a call from another designer who also offered her a job. That designer was Ralph Lauren, whom Wang had also met while she was working at *Vogue*. Lauren was asking her to work for him as a design director.

"He offered me four times [the salary] I'd ever had in my life, so I took it," said Wang. But Geoffrey Beene was not happy about her decision. "It was very hard on me because I idolized Geoffrey, and he never spoke to me again," remembered Wang. "But I had to have some money. I was thirty-eight years old, and I was still living off my parents. But he didn't understand."

In 1987 Wang began working for Ralph Lauren. As a design director, she was responsible for thirteen different lines (designs in a particular group or category) of Ralph Lauren accessories. Lauren also gave her the chance to design sportswear and lingerie. Wang loved the fact that

IN FOCUS

Ralph Lauren: Nimble Innovator

Born in 1939 in New York, Ralph Lauren has shaped his many clothing innovations around classy but casual style. He started in the fashion industry as a glove and tie salesman. In the late 1960s, he developed wide tie designs under the Polo brand that initially didn't catch on. But by the 1980s, Lauren's sense of style came to define the male office worker who wanted his clothes to look contemporary but powerful. Lauren's lines later came to include women's clothing, linens, and furniture. And his Polo retail outlets continue to push the brand forward worldwide.

Fashion guru: Ralph Lauren (shown here in about 1970) brought casual class to men's wear.

her job allowed her to express her own creativity. She also admired the classic elegance and high quality of Ralph Lauren's products. But she still longed to design her own line of clothing.

Occasionally, Vera worked up the nerve to speak to her father again about loaning her enough money to start her own business. One day she told him about an idea that she had been brainstorming—a new line of dresses and tops, designed by her. She planned to call it Ship to Shore. But once again, her father did not feel that she was ready to start her own business. Vera was disappointed, but she had no intention of giving up on her dreams.

Destiny Calls

In 1987, seven years after first meeting Arthur Becker, Wang ran into him again. And once again, he asked her to go on a date. This time Wang considered accepting Becker's offer. He was attractive, she thought. And she felt as if she had room in her life for a relationship. She agreed to the date but said she would pick the restaurant. Becker was thrilled. "Either she'd gotten smarter, or I'd gotten more interesting," Arthur Becker later joked.

When Becker showed up for the date, he had a big surprise. He arrived at the restaurant to find Wang and her whole family there to meet him. Becker felt a little nervous. But he would soon understand why Wang invited her family on the date. "That's Vera. She has a strong sense of family, and of how things go together, of what the obligations are," said Becker.

Becker was a friendly, hardworking man, and Wang's family took a liking to him. Wang was drawn to him too. And as the couple spent more time together, they swiftly fell in love. Later that year, Becker proposed to Wang on a romantic getaway golf vacation in Kukuihaele, a small town on the Hamakua coast of Hawaii. The proposal was hurried—as Wang later wrote, there was "no bended knee. No ring. No nothing. . . . Even though this was not how I had envisioned my proposal would be, I said yes."

Paradise proposal: Becker proposed to Wang during a romantic vacation on the Hamakua coast *(above)* in Hawaii. Wang accepted even though he hadn't proposed romantically enough to suit her.

That first proposal was not the end of the story, though. Wang said, "I finally got my formal proposal. And it was as sentimental and romantic as the one I had once longed for, and filled with just the right amount of hysteria. During dinner with close friends, Arthur arranged for my engagement ring to be placed in a piece of my favorite cake. As it didn't take long for me to eat dessert, Arthur immediately began to panic. As he leaned over to examine what was left on my plate, my eye caught a slight glimmer of metal. At that instant, I knew. Reaching over to hug him, I was genuinely filled with happiness and hope for what would be our future."

Wedding Bells

The couple set a wedding date for June 1989. As Wang began planning for the big event, she started to hunt for a fashionable bridal gown. For three months, she searched boutiques and stores in New York, looking for the perfect wedding dress. Wang's parents, who were excited about their daughter's upcoming marriage, encouraged her to spare no expense on her wedding gown. But the task of finding the perfect dress did not prove to be easy. Too many of the styles that Wang saw looked the same to her— an off-the-shoulder design with a traditional full skirt, banded sleeves, and beaded with sequins. This kind of dress seemed more appropriate for a younger bride, thought Wang. Why were there no dresses for older brides? At thirty-nine years old, Wang wanted a dress that was elegant, simple, and mature but also pretty and romantic.

Finally, Wang gave up trying to find a dress in a store. With financial help from her parents, she decided to design her own gown. Wang spent many hours sketching designs. When she finally had one that she liked, she hired a highly

Frustrated: The wedding gowns Wang could find suited a woman much younger than her nearly forty years. Yards of fabric were usually covered in frilly flounces, bows, and beads—a style for a young bride. As time went on, Wang grew frustrated.

skilled dressmaker to sew it. In the end, Wang's gown was streamlined and glamorous. Decorated with elaborate, expensive beadwork, the finished dress cost ten thousand dollars to create and weighed 25 pounds (11 kilograms). "I didn't really like [the dress]," Wang admitted of her final design. "But it was all even I knew of bridal at the time."

Five days before her fortieth birthday, in front of four hundred guests, Wang walked down the aisle. As was traditional, her four bridesmaids wore identical dresses. The women, all businesswomen around her age, felt silly being dressed in the same outfit. "It was very

Second chance: Many years after first meeting Arthur Becker *(left)*, Wang started to date him seriously. Within a few months, they were engaged. During her search for a perfect wedding dress that suited her style, Wang found her first design niche—bridal.

difficult. They kept saying they felt like the Supremes," Wang later said. (The Supremes were a popular female musical group in the 1960s and 1970s whose members usually wore matching costumes.)

In Chinese tradition, a new bride is supposed to wear pink and red after her wedding ceremony. So after the ceremony, Wang changed into a simple, lightweight, pale pink dress. She was happy to get out of her heavy white gown.

Wang's search for a wedding dress had not been a positive experience. After her wedding, she started thinking about the need for elegant, modern wedding designs for women of all ages.

In China the color red stands for good luck, happiness, joy, vitality, and long life. Pink is also a favored color that denotes love and romance.

An Important Decision

Wang and her husband both wanted to have children. Because they were both already nearing middle age, they decided not to wait. The newlyweds tried to get pregnant right away. But after six months, Wang still could not conceive. She began to wonder if the stress of her job at Ralph Lauren was preventing a pregnancy. After talking it over with her husband, she decided to quit her job.

"It was a difficult decision, but I couldn't try to get pregnant and carry the workload," said Wang. "We were determined to be parents." Wang began taking fertility drugs. But still, she couldn't conceive. She was deeply disappointed. She wanted very much to have children— but this apparently wasn't the time, she thought. She felt restless and bored. She just wasn't used to being unemployed. And she began to worry about her decision to leave the fashion business to focus on becoming a mom.

That was when Wang's father surprised her. After years of urging her to wait before going into the design industry, he suddenly changed his mind. Wang recalled, "All those years, it was, would you pay for design school? No. Would you help me do a blouse business? No. Finally, there I was at Ralph, 40 years old and trying to get pregnant, and [my father] said, 'Hey, why don't you start your own business?' I said, 'What, are you joking? I don't want to do it.' And he said, 'Now is the right time, because you don't want to do it. You won't be so emotional.' Isn't that bizarre? . . . And then he said, 'Bridal.' I said, 'Are you kidding? I don't want to do bridal. It's a commodity. It's not fashion.'" Wang went on, "I mean, that I should end up in bridal . . . I might as well have been doing scuba equipment."

Dad's surprise: Wang's father *(left)* had long been hesitant about her fashion industry goals. But he surprised her in early 1990 when he encouraged her to start her own business. He offered to loan her money to do it, and he even suggested that bridal might be a good focus. After giving the idea some thought, Wang realized she had some new ideas about bridal that just might catch on.

But then, remembering her own frustrating experience buying a wedding dress, Wang realized that she had valuable ideas about bridal wear. "I wanted to go into an area where I could make a real contribution," said Wang. "I think most of the great houses that I admire have done that: Chanel was always that cardigan jacket, Armani was the deconstructed suit and Ralph Lauren was about an American . . . sportswear sense of life. Every house that I know of started with one thing . . . for me, it would be wedding."

Wang soon told her friend Ralph Lauren about her plan to become a designer. He knew Wang had talent, and he wished her well. "He believed in me," she later said.

Not everyone had such confidence in her plan, however. Around the same time, another famous designer spoke with Wang. Calvin Klein had heard that she didn't have a job, and he had offered her a job working for him. But Wang explained that she wanted to design her own line of bridal gowns. "Calvin thought I was crazy," remembered Wang, "saying that when the bridal thing doesn't work, give me a call."

But Wang was not about to allow someone else's opinion to get in her way. She knew in her heart that she could be a successful fashion designer. And she was determined to give it her best.

CHAPTER FOUR

Giant leap: Looking pensive, Wang poses among drawings, dress forms, and fabric after opening the Vera Wang Bridal House.

On Her Own

About one year after her June 1989 wedding, Vera Wang took a giant leap. Borrowing $4 million from her father, she rented a two-story shop space in the elegant Carlyle Hotel in Manhattan. She renovated and redecorated the store, and she hired Chet Hazzard—a friend of hers and a former employee of designer Anne Klein—to help her launch the brand-new business.

In September 1990, Wang and Hazzard opened Vera Wang Bridal House Ltd. Wang was practical. She did plan to design her own bridal wear. But first, she wanted to get her store off the ground. So Wang filled her shop with wedding dresses by designers who were already popular, including Carolina Herrera, Pat Kerr, and Helen Benton. The average price for a wedding gown in Wang's shop was about thirty-five hundred dollars.

Like many first-time business owners, Wang discovered that running her own shop was not easy. Business was very slow at first. "I couldn't have picked a worse time to start my business," Wang later said. "It was four days before the Gulf War, in 1990, and right before a recession. . . . But that's the double-edged sword . . . the excitement and the fear of working in a gut-wrenching business."

Luckily, Wang had support from friends. Her former coworkers at *Vogue* published a six-page article that praised her budding business. News of Vera Wang Bridal House traveled fast.

While Wang's life was busy and exciting, she still felt that something was missing. She and husband still wanted to have children. The fertility treatments hadn't worked, and they weren't able to conceive a baby on their own. In 1991 Wang and Arthur adopted a baby girl. They named her Cecilia. "We weren't stuck on giving birth," said Wang. "We just wanted a family."

Providing a Service

Meanwhile, Wang's bridal shop began to thrive. The business did well partly because it was unique. She not only offered her customers a wide selection of unusual, well-made bridal gowns, but she also provided them with a valuable service.

"After a dress is delivered, Wang's stylists sit down with the future bride and consult on everything from jewelry, gloves and shoes to how she should wear her hair," said one business reporter. "Advice on flowers . . . bridesmaids' dresses, even the ceremony, is not uncommon."

Wang understood firsthand that a bride-to-be needs help organizing her wedding. "If I'm going to open a store, it's going to be about finding the other Veras that are running around looking for special dresses, looking to have everything taken care of because they have busy lives," Wang said.

Business slowly began to improve. In 1992, her second year in business, Wang sold close to one thousand wedding gowns. She took in sales of about $3 million. Despite her popularity, Wang still hadn't made a profit, and she remained deeply in debt from starting up the shop. But Wang knew that she just had to be patient and give her new business time to grow. She had worked too hard to give up.

Introducing Vera Wang

By 1994 Vera Wang Bridal House was officially making a profit. Wang and business partner Hazzard

Good enough?: Wang stares at one of her wedding dress designs in the early 1990s.

felt the time was right for Wang to launch her own designs.

Vera divided her designs into two separate markets: ready-to-wear and couture. Her factory-made, ready-to-wear (also called off-the-rack) dresses sold for between two thousand and ten thousand dollars. Her couture, one-of-a-kind gowns, on the other hand, sold for thirty thousand dollars or even more.

Customers quickly fell in love with Wang's designs. "She balanced fashion edginess with traditional elegance," said Hazzard. Wang took the formal qualities of typical wedding wear—such as the use of fine, luxurious fabrics—and combined them with the casual simplicity of sportswear.

Haute Couture

Haute couture is a French phrase that means "high design" or "high fashion." (Literally, *haute* means "high," and couture means "sewing" or "dressmaking.") Haute couture clothing is made to order for a specific customer, and usually only wealthy people can afford the artistry, time, and high-quality fabric needed to create these items. Most haute couture garments are made in the fashion capitals of the world, such as London, England; Milan, Italy; Paris, France; and New York City.

Making a haute couture gown is very time-consuming work. But Wang has always loved paying close attention to the details and careful work needed for a couture garment. She brought this quality to the saffron yellow gown she made for actress Michelle Williams. After making hundreds of sketches and working personally with the actress, Wang chose a final design for the dress. Then the gown was painstakingly cut and fit to Williams's body, using a mock-up fabric rather than the final cloth. At last, a skillful seamstress constructed the chiffon and tulle gown, which had a deep neckline and dramatic ruffles.

All of this work can take more than one hundred hours. And a gown with extra accent—one embellished with thousands of hand-sewn beads, for example—could take thousands of hours or even more.

Say it with saffron: The details tell the story in this saffron gown worn by actress Michelle Williams at the Academy Awards.

By taking old styles and making them look fresh and original, Wang created a new look in bridal that was entirely her own. One way she made her mark was with color. Traditionally, bridal gowns were almost always white or off-white. "White is wonderful for a majority of weddings because it's symbolic . . . it's hopeful and it's positive and clean, and most women look incredible in white, depending on the tone," Wang explained. But she wanted to offer brides more options. Wang experimented by making entire bridal lines in pale pink, green, and

Finally famous: Vera Wang's bridal gowns have become so well known that they have appeared in museums as part of bridal exhibits.

Riding a wave: Wang poses with three fashion models wearing her bridal ·
designs in the late 1990s.

blue. For more unconventional brides, she offered solid-color dresses
in these hues. A bride with more traditional tastes, on the other hand,
could wear a classic white dress adorned with colored trim. "I was the
first to really bring color to weddings," said Wang.

And, as always, Wang continued to provide high-quality, one-on-
one assistance to busy brides-to-be. Vera Wang and her staff "are very
knowledgeable," said one shopper. "They don't push anything on you,
but they really know the dresses well and make them fit perfectly."

Wang's experience as a retail saleswoman, as well as her own experience getting married, prepared her for selling bridal wear. "To dress women," Wang later joked, "you are part psychiatrist and part mother figure."

Good press also helped Wang's business. Reporters from influential publications such as *People* magazine and the *New York Times* gave Vera Wang positive reviews. They spoke of the fine fabrics she used to make her gowns. They wrote about her exquisite attention to detail, such as the intricate beadwork found on many Vera Wang creations.

With her shop riding a wave of success, Wang soon introduced other designs. She opened a special shop in a hotel suite across the street from her wedding boutique. There, she offered unique haute couture designs that were not bridal. Wang also began using her Vera Wang Bridal House boutique to market her wedding dresses to high-end department stores, such as Saks Fifth Avenue and Barneys New York.

For the first five years she was in business, Wang didn't participate in fashion shows of her work. Instead, she and Hazzard poured their resources and energy into building factories. "You can't work with expensive white fabrics around machines covered with oil," said Hazzard. "So we built our factories like pharmaceutical plants. Impeccable."

A Terrifying Event

Vera Wang was excited. Her new business was steadily improving. Happy customers told their friends about Wang's unique gowns and her helpful bridal service. Meanwhile, Wang's mind raced with new designs. Whenever she had a free moment, she sketched in her drawing pad.

On March 23, 1994, twenty-two-year-old bride-to-be Alisa Schaeffer was shopping at Vera Wang Bridal House. Shopping with Alisa were her parents, Gerald and Edith Schaeffer, a wealthy Maryland couple, and her fourteen-year-old sister, Jennifer. Suddenly, two men entered the shop and demanded that Gerald Schaeffer hand over his wallet. When Schaeffer refused to give the men his money, one of the robbers shot him in the stomach. The second gunman grabbed the gun and pointed it at Edith. He ordered her to take off her sixty-thousand-dollar, six-and-one-half carat diamond ring and hand it over. Edith struggled to slide the ring off her finger. Growing impatient, the robber grabbed her arm to pull the ring forcibly off her finger. As the ring slid off, he shot her in the stomach.

The attackers who had charged into Vera Wang's shop escaped that day, but they were later caught and sent to prison. And while the Schaeffers were seriously injured, they survived the brutal robbery. Nevertheless, it was a terrifying incident that would haunt Wang for years. She later called the shooting "one of the most upsetting events that has happened to me in my . . . years in this business."

Although not at the salon when the attack happened, Wang offered twenty-five thousand dollars as a reward for the robbers' capture. They were caught and tried. The judge sentenced both men to long stays in prison. Randy Caggiano, the main assailant, got thirty-six years. Sandor Sebok got twenty-eight years.

Applause: Wang gives her models a round of applause after a showing of her wedding fashions in New York.

Glamorous Gowns

Despite the highly publicized shooting, customers continued to flock to Wang's shop. As her popularity grew, Wang wanted to expand into new lines. At first Wang designed bridesmaid collections. She also designed dramatic evening wear.

Wang was admired for her unique work with evening wear—such as the "illusion fabric" sewn into some formal gowns that (at a distance) appears to be the wearer's skin. "I'm always looking for another way to look at evening wear. It's the section of a woman's closet where she will spend the most money," Wang told *In Style* magazine writer Hal Rubenstein. "And it's where she can make her biggest mistakes; going for glamour that's too old-fashioned . . . too busy, too heavy."

Women loved Wang's gowns because they were glamorous and finely made. Wang typically used luxurious fabrics, such as duchess satin, tulle, and velvet. Many customers, once they put on a Vera Wang gown, felt wonderful. Writer Adena Halpern described in the magazine *Marie Claire* how a Vera Wang gown helped her get through a breakup with her boyfriend. "I didn't buy [the gown] to wear in public. I bought it for those sad nights. . . . Whenever I got beyond depressed . . . I would put on that dress . . . and frolic around my apartment until I felt

The Importance of Fabric

Wang once commented on her view of various fabrics. "I love jersey. Silk, matte viscose, all of it. You can trust it because it adds no bulk and it drapes with no weight. All fluid fabrics like chiffon and georgette are great. And tulle. With a petticoat it gets all stiff and ladylike, yet over a chiffon slip it collapses into a silhouette just short of trashy. It gives me ideas."

What are these fabrics and where do they come from? Jersey is a soft, knitted fabric that was first produced on the island of Jersey off the coast of Great Britain. Viscose is supple and drapes well. The name comes from the Latin word *viscosus*, meaning "viscous, or thick and gluey." Chiffon, from the French word *chiffe* (rag), is lightweight, sheer, and wears well. French dressmaker Georgette de la Plante gave her name to a thin silk fabric. The gauzy weave of Tulle fabric—often used for veils—comes from the French town of Tulle, where it was first made in the mid-1700s.

Vera and velvet: Actress Sharon Stone turned heads in a Vera Wang design made of velvet. Wang accentuated Stone's form and figure using the smooth fabric.

better. I'd talk on the phone, watch television, . . . play video games on my computer, pay my bills, and do my laundry, all in that Vera Wang gown."

The Vera Wang Look

How has Wang created her signature look? "The magic [of making a gown fit well] is in weightless cloth, treating beading as texture, cutting armholes that add grace," Wang explained. "Cleverly exposing the best parts and sensuously draping fabric over less fabulous ones, offering enough internal support to allow a woman freedom to show off while being totally comfortable." Wang added. "Because a woman is never sexier than when she's comfortable in her clothes. That's it. End of story."

Eventually, Wang began to design ready-to-wear fashions. Wang enjoyed the practical and casual qualities of these clothes. Although wedding dresses made her famous, Wang preferred to design ready-to-wear rather than bridal or evening wear. "Ready-to-wear is what I've wanted to do since the beginning. . . . I'm not a girl who spends my life in a ball gown. Clothing is as much about lifestyle as art," said Wang.

Red Carpet Treatment

"I love the glamour of dressing a star," said Wang. "I still get excited when I see my clothes at the Oscars [Academy Awards]." Plus, providing eye-catching outfits for celebrities offers more than just excitement. "Dressing celebrities gets you noticed," says Wang. Still, her driving force is her own love of fashion. "I really do design for myself," she adds.

Rachel Weisz

Oprah Winfrey

Charlize Theron

Although Wang's designs were generally simple, they were well made and expensive. She would never substitute quality fabrics for more affordable, lower-quality material. Wang hired talented seamstresses to sew her dresses. "She's connected with the moment very well," said *Vogue* fashion news and features director Sally Singer. "Women's fashion right now isn't about conveying power and promotion and fabulosity, it's about lifestyle clothes, clothes you wear to work, wear them out and pick up your kids in them."

Wang understood that not all women have the body type of a model. "Be more accepting of your shape," she encouraged. "There are so many celebrities now... who come in so many shapes, displaying such varied ethnicity, that they should be an inspiration to everyone to see the beauty in themselves."

Exciting Times

In 1994 Wang found a new outlet for her creativity. Her friend Nancy Kerrigan, a championship figure skater, needed a costume for that year's Winter Olympics in Lillehammer, Norway. As a former skater herself, Wang understood from personal experience the importance of a skater's costume. A costume that is too heavy or tight, for instance, could make it hard to freely bend, twist, or jump. Wang also wanted to bring a new elegance and glamour to skating wear.

USA TODAY Snapshots®

America's TVs tuned to sports

Sports events with the highest television ratings of all time:

Super Bowl XVI	Jan. 24, 1982	CBS	49.1
Super Bowl XVII	Jan. 30, 1983	NBC	48.6
Winter Olympics[1]	Feb. 23, 1994	CBS	48.5
Super Bowl XX	Jan. 26, 1986	NBC	48.3
Super Bowl XII	Jan. 15, 1978	CBS	47.2

1— Broadcast included women's figure skating with Nancy Kerrigan and Tonya Harding

Source: NFL   By Ellen J. Horrow and Suzy Parker, USA TODAY, 2008

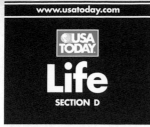

February 25, 1994

Kerrigan's costume on trial

From the Pages of
USA TODAY

Friday night the world will hold its breath as Nancy Kerrigan goes for her gold.

But perhaps no one will be more nervous than Vera Wang. The New York designer and former skater will be praying the $13,000 costume she designed for Kerrigan doesn't split, snag or ride up.

"It's my personal nightmare," says Wang.

Kerrigan will skate wearing Wang's ice couture creation, smothered with 20,000 Austrian crystals. She'll leap and spin, reflecting light like a human disco ball.

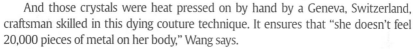

The costume is ... made of a nude stretchy fabric called Illusion. Why so expensive? Wang insists that's her cost, no markup: "The fabric alone costs $1,200 a yard."

And those crystals were heat pressed on by hand by a Geneva, Switzerland, craftsman skilled in this dying couture technique. It ensures that "she doesn't feel 20,000 pieces of metal on her body," Wang says.

Figure skating and high fashion were once contradictory terms. Until just a few years ago, figure skaters usually sported sleazy sequins, tacky tutus or lurid leotards. "When I told people I was a figure skater 15 years ago, they looked at me like I was in the circus," says Wang, 44. "No one appreciated the skater the way they do now."

Many in the sport credit her with creating the new look that has increased the sport's visual style and popularity. But designing for double axels is riskier than dressing starlets.

"When I dress an actress and she gives a bad performance, no one holds me responsible," says Wang. "But when a figure skater misses a jump, it might be because the costume didn't stretch or the crotch rode up."

—Elizabeth Snead, February 25, 1994

Kerrigan's performance won her a silver medal. But her costume also caught the attention of skating and fashion fans around the world. Kerrigan's silver and white dress glittered with fifteen hundred rhinestones. Never before had an Olympic figure skater worn something so elegant and stylish. Kerrigan's costume served as a powerful advertisement for Vera Wang.

Also in 1994, Wang and her husband welcomed another baby into their family. They adopted a second daughter, named Josephine. Wang loved being a mother. But she found the challenge of raising two young children while running a business a little daunting. "Having been a career woman, I must say that being a mother is the most challenging thing I've ever done," said Wang. "The biggest hurdle I face is lack of time."

Family of four: Vera holds Cecilia, while Arthur holds Josephine as the family of four poses in a pool.

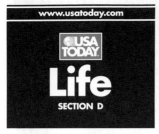

www.usatoday.com

USA TODAY.

Life

SECTION D

March 18, 1994

Many have designs on Oscar's guests

From the Pages of
USA TODAY

Vera Wang is hot. Last year, she made Oscar memories with Sharon Stone's show-stopper of a dress.

Last month, Nancy Kerrigan hit the Olympic ice in Wang designs. Monday night, Kerrigan and double nominee Holly Hunter will wear Wang to the Oscars.

The actress flew cross-country twice in a week for fittings, but the one-of-a-kind dress is strictly wait-and-see. Wang laughingly describes it as "punk-Hindu.". . . The Boss' wife, Patti Scialfa, will be in ready-to-wear. This year, Marisa Tomei's dress will be "effervescent and languorous . . . different in mood from hair to makeup to dress." [Vera] does hair? She oversees everything, "Down to the earrings and the shoes."

—Katy Kelly, March 18, 1994

Dressing the Stars

News of Vera Wang's talent also reached celebrities. Women clamored to wear her designs to well-publicized events, such as the Academy Awards, the Emmy Awards, and the Golden Globe Awards.

In 1995 actor Billy Baldwin, a hopeful groom-to-be, visited Wang's store. He planned to propose to his girlfriend, singer Chynna Phillips. He asked Wang to assist him with his wedding proposal by loaning him one hundred wedding gowns. Wang quickly agreed. "I was thrilled," she said, "because I love stories like that—very romantic."

Baldwin filled an entire room at the Carlyle Hotel with the gowns and lit the room with candles. Over caviar and champagne, he proposed to Phillips. She said yes. After the romantic proposal, bride-to-be Phillips visited Wang's bridal shop. The singer wanted a very traditional gown. Wang thought about designs. She wanted the gown to express the bride's inner and outer beauty, without being overwhelming or clunky.

Wang designed a traditional white gown with a very full skirt. She covered the bodice [chest area] of the dress with an intricate pattern of thin mother-of-pearl beads. Wang herself attended the wedding. She watched as the lovely bride walked down the aisle in a church lit only by candles. "Candlelight is beautiful any time, but less expected in a daytime wedding," said Wang. "The whole church was aglow."

In 1997 Wang introduced a new line of bridal shoes to her collection. The shoes sold for about $250 a pair. In the same year, Wang designed a wedding dress for then vice president Al Gore's daughter

Karenna and Andrew: Vice President Al Gore helps his daughter Karenna up the steps of the National Cathedral in Washington, D.C. Wang designed the wedding dress that Karenna wore at her wedding to Andrew Schiff in 1997.

Karenna, for her marriage to Andrew Schiff. "For the dress, we had a good idea: to keep it classical and minimal, with a beautiful drape," said Wang. "I wanted it to have the dignity befitting the daughter of the Vice President, but with a modern twist."

"There was perfect weather, with sunlight coming through the windows of the cathedral," said Wang about Karenna and Andrew's wedding. "It was one of the most memorable times of my life," said Wang.

In 1998 Wang and her husband had dinner with President Bill Clinton and his wife, Hillary Rodham Clinton. Also in attendance were several other interesting and prominent guests, including director Steven Spielberg and writer Amy Tan. Wang gave the First Lady a special present for the occasion—a lavender, off-the-shoulder gown.

The same year, Wang's close personal friend, actress Sharon Stone, asked her to design a wedding dress for her. Wang decided to

Hillary and Vera: Hillary Clinton wore a Vera Wang design as she and her husband, President Bill Clinton, waited to greet the Chinese president Jiang Zemin in 1998. Wang was a guest at the state dinner.

create an untraditional pink chiffon dress for Stone. The flowing gown was both glamorous and fun.

Stone had invited 120 guests to her wedding to *San Francisco Examiner* executive editor Phil Bronstein. Stone had come up with a clever idea to keep reporters and photographers away from the event. Instead of sending wedding invitations, Stone had invited her guests to a Valentine's Day party. When they arrived at the wedding hall, the guests were very surprised to find they were really attending a wedding.

While the excited guests waited in their seats for Stone to walk down the aisle, Wang was worried. Her heart raced. Her hands trembled. The pink chiffon gown was not fitting the actress's body to Wang's liking. Stone had lost a little weight since the last fitting, and the dress looked bulky around her waist. "We were literally sewing it onto Sharon's body the minute before she was going to come down the aisle," said Wang. "Sharon was cool. She had to calm me down." In the end, Stone looked lovely and the gown was a great success.

Worries for the Future

Wang knew that the fashion industry was very competitive. She knew she had to keep pushing the envelope—stretching limits of typical fashion and creating new, innovative designs and product lines—to keep her company afloat.

To promote her work, Wang put together two large trunk shows each year. A trunk show is a special sale in which a designer can sell his or her work to a specific department store or to special customers. A trunk show also allows stores to buy clothing before it is made available to the general public.

Despite the fame and success that she had already achieved, Wang continued to worry about her business. "Every night she comes home and tells me she's failing," her husband said at the time. Fortunately, Wang's worries never slowed her down. Her self-doubt only made her try even harder. Her mind was constantly creating. Even while watching television, talking with her friends, and riding in taxis, she sketched tiny figures wearing various new designs and costumes.

"She'll draw thousands of figures an inch and a half high," said her husband. Becker joked, "I have nightmares that they're going to jump off the pad and tie me up."

On the runway: *Vogue* editor Anna Wintour *(front row, far right)* watches a model in a Vera Wang design pass by during a fashion show in New York.

Busy Life

■■■■■

In April 1998, Vera Wang presented her first New York show of evening wear. It was a big event. Large fashion shows give designers the chance to present their newest lines to the press; to purchasers for stores; and to movie stars, singers, and other fans of high fashion. The largest shows are held in major style centers such as Paris, France, and Milan, Italy, as well as New York City. They feature dramatic runway shows, during which models walk up and down a narrow ramp, wearing pieces from a designer's latest collection as photographers snap pictures and fashion critics scribble notes. Those critics raved about the new Vera Wang line.

Showstopper

In 1998 actress Sharon Stone showed off her friend's designs at the Academy Awards. Stone made a strikingly bold, offbeat, glamorous "Oscar moment" when she appeared onstage to present the Oscar for Best Foreign Film. She was dressed in a lavender Vera Wang skirt topped with a crisply starched, white men's shirt.

Oscar buzz: Sharon Stone's purple Vera Wang skirt with a man's white shirt was an Oscar hit in 1998.

New Directions

As Wang's business grew and her name became more and more well known, her designs didn't stop at clothing. In 1998 she designed the Vera Wang Bride Barbie doll. She dressed the doll in an ivory satin dress trimmed in black velvet, with sleeves made of a sheer material. And, like a real Vera Wang dress, the gown was rich with details. Black velvet bows decorated the wrists, and pearly buttons flowed down the back of the dress. Wang adorned the doll bride's floor-length train with a single black velvet bow and gave her white stockings held up with a garter belt. A blue flower on the belt represented the "something blue" that a bride traditionally carries. Wang completed the look

Barbie bride: Wang designed the wedding dress for a Barbie doll in 1998.

by giving the brunette doll a simple pair of pearl earrings and a classic bouquet of red roses.

In 1999 Wang designed a second Barbie doll, this time for the Designer Barbie series. The red-haired movie star doll is dressed for an awards ceremony. She wears a flowing gown of purple satin with a deep red sash and carries a purple satin purse. The dress was part of Barbie's Salute to Hollywood Collection.

In the meantime, Wang continued to design gowns for real-life women. In 1999 she created a wedding dress for Victoria Adams—better known as Posh Spice, a member of the musical group the Spice Girls. In her wedding to soccer superstar David Beckham, "Posh wanted to be like a modern Cinderella," said Wang. "They wed in a castle with two thrones for the ceremony. Talk about fairy tales."

Wang also made a gown for Vanessa Williams, an actress, singer, and former Miss America who was married in September 1999. Before she started sketching, Wang asked Williams lots of questions about her wedding. Where was the wedding going to be held? How many people would attend? Would there be flowers—and if so, what color? Was it to be a daytime or nighttime wedding? "I always get involved in a wedding," said Wang. "Otherwise I can't design the dress. I'm a bit of a control freak if you give me a chance."

Williams told Wang that she wanted a romantic, traditional wedding. Wang got to work. She knew that Williams was both beautiful and graceful, and Wang wanted to design a dress that complemented those qualities. Wang created a dress that resembled a ballerina's dress. The dress was sleeveless, with many yards of tulle. The top of the dress was a simple, tight silk corset, with tiny bows down the back.

Vanessa and Vera: Vanessa Williams and husband Rick Fox are all smiles at their wedding in 1999. Wang worked hard to create just the right look for Williams.

"What is wonderful about the couples I've worked with is how in love they are," said Wang. "This was Vanessa's second wedding, and she wanted to look like a storybook bride for him. That's true romance."

Wang also designed a dress for Olympic figure skater Kristi Yamaguchi's July 2000 wedding. Yamaguchi planned to wed outdoors on a beach in Hawaii. Wang wanted to make the skater an elegant, cool, and casual dress that would blend with the natural surroundings. She designed a narrow, lightweight satin dress with a snug-fitting bodice. She then hired an artist to hand paint garlands of pearls and flowers on the dress. Wang also designed a tiara for Yamaguchi to wear during the ceremony.

Celebrities appreciated how Wang took special care to respect their privacy. Wang is known for her ability to hide even the most famous people's wedding plans from the press. "I think I could work for the CIA [Central Intelligence Agency]," laughed Wang.

Wang's wedding gowns are expensive—either new or used. Every gown comes with a certificate of authenticity. A person buying a secondhand Vera Wang gown should ask to see the certificate before handing over any money.

Wang on Weddings

Vera Wang's fans admire more than her designs. Customers appreciate her ability to make them look good, regardless of age or body type. "We've all got flaws, honey," Wang told a reporter. "No one has a perfect body. That's why designers still have jobs. Ninety-nine percent of the women I've dressed feel most vulnerable in the same area—the stomach," she explained. To solve this problem, Wang makes the fabric around the waist "flat and tight, and never puffy or bulky."

USA TODAY Life

SECTION D

February 11, 2002

Potential gold medalist's attire a secret

From the Pages of USA TODAY

Michelle Kwan is America's de facto first lady of figure skating. So it's no surprise that the costumes she'll don for competition are shrouded in as much secrecy as an inaugural ball gown. And like any first lady, Kwan has her design muse: fashion leader Vera Wang.

In their first Olympic collaboration, Wang has created five bejeweled outfits for the potential gold medalist, two of which Kwan will showcase when she glides into the Salt Lake Ice Center for the short and long programs next week.

"I just don't want to fail her," says Wang, who is attending her first Olympics. She will be sitting in the stands cheering— and hoping that a strap won't snap.

A former Olympic skating hopeful herself, Wang, 52, revolutionized skating costumes much in the way she transformed bridal gowns. She took ice attire from spangly get-ups that looked like they had leaped off a circus trapeze to elegant, subtle dresses that complement, rather than overwhelm, a skater's artistry.

[Wang is] adamant about the fact that these are technical garments that just happen to sparkle; on the ice, form and function are tightly knit. "Though people like to view it as something theatrical and telegenic, it really is part of their equipment. It has to fit flawlessly. In no way can it impede their athletic performance."

—Olivia Barker, February 11, 2002

Dressed for success: Michelle Kwan skates in her Vera Wang costume at the 2002 Olympics. She won the bronze medal.

Please see COVER STORY next page ►

Chet Hazzard, Wang's longtime business partner, remarked, "Vera is an intelligent, strong person, really connected to women. She understands the female form in all of its imperfections and perfections. She finds solutions by working with the body."

In 2001 Wang released her first book, *Vera Wang on Weddings*. In the book, Wang offered brides-to-be advice on all aspects of their wedding day. Wang knew that not all women could afford her pricey bridal designs. But many more brides-to-be could buy her sixty-five-dollar book. "If they can't af-

First book: Wang *(left)* celebrates the publication of her book, *Vera Wang on Weddings*, with fashion writer and socialite Helen Lee Schifter.

ford the dress, they can still take a part of me with them," said Wang.

Wang advises a bride-to-be not to experiment on her wedding day. "Your wedding day is not the time to experiment with a new hairdo, hair color, haircut or makeup. . . . When I don't recognize a bride who I've been working with for six months on her wedding day, I go into shock."

Wang had worked as a wedding-wear designer for eleven years when her book was released. Her experiences—both the positive and the negative—helped her write the book. "I have experienced bad

Details, Details

In 288 pages, *Vera Wang on Weddings* gives readers a glimpse of the level of detail to which Wang is willing to go to make every wedding memorable. Dos and Don'ts abound, from stationery to bouquets to food. Here's a sampling of Wang's advice.

- Do carefully orchestrate spontaneity.
- Don't plan a wedding until all money issues have been worked out.
- Do share gown decisions with the florist, who can then coordinate decorations and bouquets appropriately.
- Don't use a skimpy aisle runner at the service, and be sure it lies straight and flat.
- Do personalize chairs at the reception with greenery, bows, or cushions.
- Don't have only one garter. Bring one to toss and one to keep.

valet parking. I have experienced when you've set it for outdoors and everyone is frozen," said Wang. "Someone asked me if I did research on the book. I said, 'No, it's all in my head. I've lived it.'"

Hip Mom

Wang somehow manages to design new and successful fashions, run her massive company, and be a mom. Although her schedule is packed tight, Wang loves spending time with her daughters. She has shared her love of skating with them, taking them to rinks and letting them try out the sport for themselves. And just like their energetic mom, Josephine and Cecilia are creative and artistic. From an early age, whenever Wang was working at home, her daughters would sit beside her with pads of paper, scribbling their own sketches and drawings. "They copy Mom," says Becker.

Wang's two daughters go to the Chapin School, which their mother also attended in the 1950s and 1960s. Cecilia will be graduating soon, while Josephine has a few more years left before she moves on to her next adventure.

Wang learned traditional Chinese customs and behavior from her parents. She hasn't passed on many of those traditions to her daughters, however. "I'm totally Americanized, yet in many ways the feelings I have for people and the respect I have are inherently Chinese," said Wang. "I am still deferential to my parents in a way that my daughters are not to me."

Wang's daughters help keep her up to date on what's hip and trendy in the

Busy mom: Vera and her daughters Cecilia *(left)* and Josephine enjoy a night out in 2001.

fashion world. However, Wang knows that, in fashion, trends aren't necessarily new. "There's nothing 'new' in fashion," Wang once said, with her characteristic dry humor. "I've lived through bellbottoms five times."

USA TODAY

CHAPTER SEVEN

Tradition: After the presentation of a seasonal collection, the models traditionally applaud while the designer takes a bow. Here Wang gets her due after showing her spring 2003 collection in September 2002.

Totally Committed

Vera Wang is not someone who takes it easy very often. Wang's business partner, Hazzard, once called her "passionate, perfectionist and fearless. Vera is always moving, always looking." Wang's own husband calls her a "force of nature."

To get everything done, Wang follows a strict daily routine. On a typical morning, Wang sleeps in until about nine, getting to work around ten thirty. Once at the office, she works tirelessly all day at her business, without taking a break, until seven each evening. When she gets home, however, she is happy to kick back and relax with her family. She likes to get takeout or fast food and hang out in her den with her kids and husband. "We'll sit with lunches on trays, McDonald's preferably, and watch TV. It's the best," Wang says. She adds that she's a big fan of the television program *Law and Order*. "I have seen every episode there ever was," reports Wang.

But Wang's workday doesn't end when she gets home. After helping her girls with their homework and tending to household tasks, Wang goes back to work. She typically designs from eleven to two each night. "This is my quiet time," says Wang, "when I have time to really think and create."

Because of her night-owl work habits, Wang is still asleep when her kids leave for school in the morning. "I do not wake up with my kids, for which I will pay the price forever!" Wang jokes.

Fortunately, Wang's long work hours do not have a negative impact on her marriage. Becker is a busy executive, with business interests ranging from binoculars to golf equipment. "My husband's a great, great partner—as a husband and a father," says Wang. "He's also a workaholic. If I didn't have somebody who was really into his own profession, there's no way he'd put up with a wife like me."

Force of Nature

Wang is involved in all aspects of her business. She personally inspects

USA TODAY Snapshots®

Wedding spending by sector

In 2003, the average wedding cost more than $21,000. The top sectors in billions:

Receptions $16
Honeymoons $7
Engagement rings $5
Wedding gowns $2

Source: Bridal Guide InfoSource

By Darryl Haralson and Frank Pompa, USA TODAY, 2004

Nailing the details: Wang continues to take an active role in each season's fashion show. She helps finalize the look of each model before the model steps on the runway.

every item for sale in her boutiques and salons. But Wang doesn't work alone. She relies heavily on a team of trusted assistants for her clothing line. Wang oversees and delegates responsibilities to members of her two-hundred-member staff. But Wang has the final say on all products and decisions.

"I try to share a tremendous amount with my staffers," says Wang. "I feel everything: the tribulations of business, the responsibility to people who depend on me to feed their families. Those things are always in the decision-making processes."

"Vera doesn't have casual feelings about things," said her husband. "She has strong views, strong feelings. . . . And she has the ability to persist when I would have died of exhaustion long since."

Fast-talking Wang has been accused of being not only a workaholic but also intense. "Intense? Without a doubt!" says her husband. "She is totally committed to what she's doing. And like everything else, it's a blessing and a curse."

More New Directions

Wang's business is constantly growing. She is always working on new designs and exploring new product lines, dividing her time between her two New York City boutiques and her West 39th Street showroom. As much as she loves designing, Wang does not get to spend all of her time doing that part of her job. She also has to attend business meetings and fashion photo shoots, appear on television, and give interviews to the press.

Sometimes Wang herself feels pulled in too many directions. But, she says, "What keeps me going is a passion and a love for what I do."

She is very hands on with her business—such as with the Vera Wang beauty cream she released in 2002. "For the body cream, she insisted it's important how it feels when you put your hand in the jar," recalls Hazzard. "So she wanted no ridge around the rim to interfere with the sensuality of the experience."

Vera and the media: Wang makes herself available to the press during fashion shows. Having good relations with the media is an important part of her company's success.

September 11, 2003

More than meets the eye

From the Pages of
USA TODAY

Famous wedding gown designer Vera Wang used the sidelines of Monday's Philadelphia-Tampa Bay game as a runway to debut the new outfits she created for the Eagles cheerleaders. Language can be inadequate in conveying the essence of fashion. But one can try, always try: Think hot pants and a Wonderbra and, hmm, that's about it. Perhaps most important, Wang argues the cheerleaders' outfits "in no way impede their athletic performance."

—September 11, 2003

New look: The cheerleaders for the NFL's Philadelphia Eagles show off their new costumes designed by Vera Wang.

Wang's family was very wealthy. Her thriving business has made her rich in her own right. "She could stay home and eat canapés," says one reporter. "She could have made dresses for friends. She could have done nothing. Instead, she's taken on the world."

Vera Wang strives to keep her company strong, prosperous, and ever expanding. But that doesn't mean she is less concerned about creating a fine product than when she first started as a designer. "At the company, we walk a fine line between being commercial and being creative," said Wang. "We want most to be respected."

Wang acknowledges that many challenges exist in the world of fashion. She can't produce every interesting design she creates, for instance. "You have to make compromises because the most cutting-edge things are not necessarily what sells. You have to find a balance; it's a very difficult thing to do." But Vera Wang has clearly struck a balance. Her business has grown by leaps and bounds since she first launched the company in 1990.

Rest and Relaxation

In her rare free time, Wang likes to read and play golf. And somewhat surprisingly for a woman who is known for her high energy and long work hours, Wang says that she is also a "big believer in sleeping, which I think heals your psyche."

Wang was named to a list of female celebrity golfers compiled by *Golf for Women* magazine. Her handicap, a numerical measure of an amateur golfer's playing ability, was estimated at 28. The lower the handicap, the better the player is. The winning celebrity, singer Anne Murray, has an estimated 11 handicap.

Wang also loves to travel for both work and pleasure. On business she has traveled to faraway places, such as Italy, France, China, and India. On these "sourcing trips," Wang collects things that inspire her work, such as bolts of Italian wool and satin from Shanghai.

Wang also likes to shop for fun when she travels. She collects unusual things, such as interesting toothpaste, that she finds on her trips. Her favorite place to buy toothpaste is Antica Farmacia Santa Maria della Scala, an old-fashioned drugstore in Rome, Italy. And Wang says that she has "a huge chopstick collection," with finds from all over the world.

Of course, Wang also loves to shop for clothes, and she has many special treasures in her closet. One of her most prized possessions is a Prada crocodile coat. The coat is one of only four like it in the world. "My closet is the Harvard Business School of Fashion," jokes Wang. "I love owning, studying or wearing the designer who does something the best. If you don't know who does what best, it's very hard to know if what you're doing is good."

The Sweet Smell of Success

Wang works to constantly move her company in new and exciting directions. "There isn't room in fashion today for little businesses," she says. Not everyone has to be a top designer like Ralph Lauren or Calvin Klein, she clarifies. "But it's a question of survival. . . . It's grow or die, as they say on Wall Street. It's about the bottom line. Anybody who says it isn't, isn't really in the business."

In 2002, with that business philosophy in mind, Wang released a perfume for women. Called Vera Wang Eau de Parfum, the fragrance is a mixture of rose, calla lily, and mandarin flower scents, with a touch of lotus, gardenia, iris, and musk. "It's soft and voluptuous and smells like white flowers," said one fan. One woman who smelled the perfume asked, "Is this what marital bliss smells like?" Wang was thrilled when her perfume for women won the FiFi Award in 2003.

Vera Wang's Favorite Designers

Vera Wang loves fashion. As Paul Cavaco, a former coworker of Vera's and the creative director of *Allure* magazine, put it, "Vera loves clothes beyond loving clothes; she loves everything that has to do with clothes. This is not a make-believe love here; it's the real thing."

So, not surprisingly, Wang's closets are overflowing with gorgeous—and extremely expensive—designer clothing. While she has collected chic and fashionable clothing her whole life, she usually dresses quite casually. Her favorite outfit is a simple, loose shirt or shift with her trademark black leggings from the Gap. The look is clean, elegant, and very "Vera."

Wang has many favorite designers. A few of the labels in her closets include Miuccia Prada, Yves Saint Laurent, Jil Sander, Yohji Yamamoto, Louis Vuitton, Jean Paul Gaultier, and Ann Demeulemeester. "I think I have spent a serious fortune on clothes in my life," says Wang. "I probably could have owned more paintings and sculpture had I not bought all the clothing. It's my passion."

"Couture—I love it. But by definition it almost means 'important to own, important to wear.'. . . I prefer work by someone like Miuccia Prada, which is so beautifully made and has rich details. . . . No one wears only me. Not even me!"

Miuccia Prada

Yohji Yamamoto

FiFi award: Wang accepts an award for her perfume for women, called Vera Wang, at the Fragrance Foundation awards ceremony. She had signed a contract in 2000 with Unilever—an international vendor of food, home furnishings, and beauty products—to make a signature perfume. Within two years, the fragrance had won a major award.

Given out by the Fragrance Foundation, the FiFis are the Academy Awards of perfume. They honor creativity and achievement in the fragrance industry.

In January 2004, Wang added fine jewelry to her great variety of product lines. And the very next month, Wang ventured into new territory by creating a product specifically for male customers. Her new fragrance, Vera Wang for Men, was made with the earthy smells of nutmeg, leather, sandalwood, and other natural scents. Wang later added more fragrances for women, including Bouquet, Truly Pink, and Flower Princess.

designs, 8D
Sweet
Butterflies
success
home office: $199.86
priceless)

Always a Risk

In 2003 Wang agreed to design a wedding dress for singer and actress Jennifer Lopez, who was engaged to actor and playwright Ben Affleck. Wang duly created and delivered the dress on time. Alas, a few days before the wedding, the couple canceled. Lopez didn't pay for the gown. Scroll down to 2004, when Lopez marries singer Marc Anthony. The bride wore a champagne-colored Chantilly lace dress from Wang's spring collection. Asked if the dress was the same, a Wang publicist said "no comment."

In the meantime, Vera Wang licensed the Vera Wang name to sell many other products. Licensing links a brand name to goods that are not necessarily created by the owner of the original brand. As a result of licensing, the Vera Wang label appears on products including fur, eyewear, flatware, and accessories for the table. Wang continued to prove that her company would definitely grow, not die.

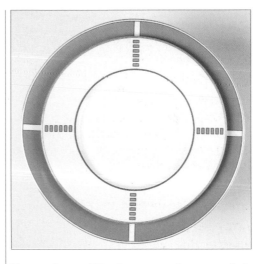

Vera at home: Wang's company has expanded into china *(above)* and flatware.

www.usatoday.com

USA TODAY

CHAPTER EIGHT

Back to Shanghai: In 2005 Wang visited the large city of Shanghai with her father, who had left the city in the 1940s. Shanghai had become one of China's largest urban areas, with a crowded shopping area.

Scaling New Heights

Vera Wang is at the height of her career. But she still sometimes worries that her business will fail. "I feel pressure that I don't think I felt as much in earlier years," says Wang. "As you become more high profile, you have more to lose."

Wang has faced real loss in her personal life. In January 2004, her mother passed away. Just over a year later, her longtime business partner Chet Hazzard died. Wang dealt with these sad events, in part, by doing what she always does—throwing herself into her work.

Full Circle

In November 2005, Wang visited China with her father. She's increasingly proud of the expansion of her business to her parents' home country. For many years, the Chinese government did not allow foreign businesses to open stores in the country. Eventually, the restrictions eased. As a result, in 2005 Wang opened a bridal store in Shanghai's Pudong Shangri-La Hotel. The boutique, called The Perfect Wedding, features Wang's creations in soft, pastel colors and traditional wedding whites. Meanwhile, Wang was happy to receive the China Fashion Award as International Fashion Designer of the Year. Wang was the first Chinese American fashion designer to win the award.

Wang also enjoyed seeing the sights of Shanghai, one of China's largest cities, with her father. "He showed me the tradition, the Ming empire, what another China was," says Wang. "I saw modern China. I expected bicycles and Mao suits [a style of suit worn by Chinese men in the early 1900s] and what I saw was a . . . China with a hunger for Western culture. It is a wonderfully exciting period.

"America brought me freedom and gave me freedom as a woman," said Wang. "In America we think anything is possible. The Chinese feel they have to work to deserve it. America gives you ease and nonchalance, which is what I try to do in my clothes." In China, Wang feels a return to her roots and the sense that her family had come full circle. "This is a very big deal for me emotionally," says Wang. "It really is my roots."

Conflicted

Sometimes Wang feels conflicted about the way she spends her workdays. Instead of doing what she loves—designing—she spends a lot of time just managing her business. "At times it has sapped my enthusiasm," Wang confesses.

Even as she takes on more tasks and responsibilities, Wang continues to use her hands-on approach to business. She personally oversees all projects and items that bear her famous name. Wang is constantly juggling projects and striving to accomplish her many goals.

"I marvel at her ability to handle it all," said Wang's longtime friend Lisa Jackson. "She likes to stay home, have dinner, have some laughs and watch TV. With family and friends, she's very steady." Wang knows she needs more free time. "It would be nice to just have a cup of Starbucks and read a magazine. That really is the time that I don't have," said Wang.

Some people, including her best friends, consider Wang to be a perfectionist. But Wang doesn't necessarily agree. "I'm not Martha Stewart," Wang said. "I'm not going to tell you how to make your cupcakes—if you don't even want . . . cupcakes, that's okay."

 Wang recently allowed a rare glimpse of her attention to detail in a commercial for Hewlett-Packard (HP), the hardware computer manufacturer. Through miniatures, viewers saw her sweep from watching her children ice skate to pushing a bride and groom into a color-coordinated honeymoon car to choosing music for her runway shows.

Hawaiian Suite

Wang tried yet another new direction in 2005, when she designed the Vera Wang Suite at the Halekulani Hotel in Honolulu, Hawaii. It is a wedding suite for honeymoons and other romantic occasions. "Vera Wang has stayed at some of the world's most exotic locations," said Peter Shaindlin, the head of the Halekulani company. "Her sensibility is international, and she has exquisite taste you can trust absolutely."

Showoff: The Vera Wang Suite at the Halekulani Hotel in Hawaii shows off Wang's taste in linen, furniture, crystal, and even movies for late-night viewing.

The suite also displays many Vera Wang items, including linens, fine crystal and china, and throw pillows custom-trimmed with wedding dress scraps. While other rooms at the hotel are painted white, Wang wanted to liven up her rooms with color. Yet she didn't want the color to overpower, or take away from, the striking natural colors of the Hawaiian scenery. Inspired by Hawaii's exotic tropical flowers, Wang chose to paint the suite lavender, pale green, and orange red persimmon. The suite rents for between four thousand and fifty-five hundred dollars per night.

The suite also shows off a display case filled with Vera Wang crystal and porcelain designed for Wedgwood (a company that makes traditional fine china and crystal). Wang's company recommends these items as being perfect for wedding presents.

Family Life

Wang says her daughters, Josephine and Cecilia, handle the pressures of having a famous, workaholic mother well. "They have a good sense of humor—they have no choice!" Wang says with a laugh.

How does Wang see her many roles? "First of all, I'd define myself as a businesswoman," says Wang. "Then [a] mother. And I say this after businesswoman because the financial responsibilities are so overwhelming in my mind and I regard my own security, and that of my family, as very much interwoven in my business."

Wang's role as wife usually ends up coming last. But fortunately, she has an understanding mate. However, Wang's husband sometimes wishes that she could get a reality check—about herself. Says Becker, "[I wish] she could somehow accept the respect for her capabilities and talent that people have for her. That's the thing about people who

Growing up: In different ways, Becker and Wang are very involved with every aspect of their daughters' lives.

strive: they just keep striving. I'd like her to have the sense of satisfaction, of pleasure, of being at ease with herself."

Becker also thought of a smart way to help his busy wife relax. One Valentine's Day, Becker bought Wang a massage chair. "He knows I love massages," said Wang. "So instead of, say, getting my masseuse to come for a week, he bought me a wonderful massage chair." "I try to fulfill my husbandly duties," said Becker with a laugh.

Wang and her family have lived in several apartments in New York City. Their current apartment has fourteen rooms. The family often spends weekends or short vacations at their beach house in Southampton, Long Island, east of New York City. The family's very favorite getaway is at Pound Ridge, only a forty-five-minute drive from New York City. Wang helped to design this home, working with architect George van Geldern. Together they planned three connected stone buildings. The home is located on a large, beautiful lake, where the family likes to go swimming, fishing, and boating in the summer. In the winter, Wang and her kids ice-skate on the frozen lake. "I never relax in Manhattan . . . up here [I can] finally take a breath. A weekend here is as valuable as a month somewhere else."

Before Wang's father died in 2006, she and her extended family would go to Villa Tranquilla in Palm Beach, Florida. After the elder Wang's death, the family put the property up for sale for $23 million.

So what does Wang look for in a home? Besides beautiful architecture, lots of light, and high ceilings—a large closet is of top importance to Wang. She has an enormous—and constantly growing—clothing collection. In her New York City apartment, Wang has a closet that is 300 square feet (28 square meters) in area—as large as a small apartment. A crystal chandelier hangs overhead.

Wang is attached to every piece of clothing she owns. Each item in her closet is an old friend. "Every piece tells a story. They're like actors in a role. I know and talk to them. It's really insane. I'll say, 'I haven't worn you in a while, so I'm going to wear you again.'"

IN FOCUS

Shopping Tips from Vera

• Focus on accessories. An accessory—such as a scarf, a handbag, or shoes—can completely change a look. And they don't take up a lot of room in your closet.

• Unless you are purchasing a bathing suit, yoga clothing, or ski clothes, buy loose-fitting garments. Loose clothing fits the body best.

• If you really like something—buy two.

The Bad with the Good

Even a designer as successful and respected as Vera Wang receives bad reviews now and then. For example, some fashion writers criticized Wang's show at Bryant Park in Manhattan. "There's a fine line between gothic romance and doom and gloom," said a reporter for the *Toronto Star* newspaper in September 2005. "Vera Wang's spring [2006] collection crossed it. Wang seemed to want to play on this fall's Victoriana trend [influenced by the late nineteenth-century Victorian era in Great Britain]. . . . There were taffeta painter shirts, lace bed jackets . . . eyelet smocks, which all sounds pleasant enough except that there were too many layers, bunched ruffles . . . and pleats. The gentleness prevalent on other runways was missing here."

Yet, around the same time, another writer raved about Wang's 2006 looks. "May I introduce you to the current object of my obsession—the Vera Wang embroidered velvet cuff," wrote fashion critic Kate Reardon in a November 2005 edition of British newspaper the *Times*. "[The cuff] is perfect: just a simple piece of velvet that you knot around your wrist, beautifully embroidered with gold thread, beads

Picks and pans: Reactions varied to Wang's spring 2006 collection (which was shown in September 2005). Some fashion critics thought the collection was old and gloomy, and some thought it was classic and opulent.

and 'gems.' It's glamorous and opulent—so perfect for the party season, yet the fact that you just tie it on makes it casual enough to wear with jeans." And that year, Wang was also honored at the Council of Fashion Designers of America awards as best women's wear designer.

Wang finds inspiration for her designs from many places. She describes her spring 2006 line as being "all about [the artist Henri] Matisse." That year's fall designs were inspired by Flemish painters and featured velvet separates and soft, floating fabrics in earthy greens, golds, and browns. Dancers clothing and Japanese styles made their mark on her spring 2007 collection, which included comfortable warm-up pants and embroidered kimono jackets. Czarist Russia

Fall 2006 fashion: Wang based her fall 2006 line on the color and feel of Flemish paintings.

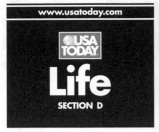

March 6, 2006

Winning look is 'luminous'

From the Pages of
USA TODAY

[Of the 2006 Oscars], *Glamour* magazine's Suze Yalof Schwartz says those who "did do it right really made a fashion statement and were absolutely luminous." [Among] her top five picks [was Best Actress nominee] Keira Knightley.

The *Pride & Prejudice* star . . . wore a single-strapped Vera Wang gown that "fits her unbelievably," Yalof Schwartz says. "I love her hair pulled back in a ponytail, the smoky eye with the pale lip. She is the most gorgeous, glamorous actress of the night."

—Donna Freydkin, March 6, 2006

Stunning: Keira Knightley wowed the fans and the fashion crowd with her deep maroon, off-the-shoulder Vera Wang gown.

provided the inspiration for her fall 2007 line, which many viewers called pioneering, with military-inspired detailing and knee-high boots. Ancient Rome brought punch to her spring 2008 collection, which was filled with vibrantly colored satins that fluidly spun down the runway. And glittering tassels were a prominent design element of her fall 2008 line.

International influence: Japanese style inspired Wang for her spring 2007 collection *(upper left)*. For fall 2007 *(upper right)*, Wang looked to czarist Russia. Spring 2008 *(bottom left)* had a twist of ancient Rome, and in fall 2008 *(bottom right)*, Wang went for glitz, glamour, and tassles.

IN F⊙CUS

A Huge Loss

In September 2006, on the morning of Wang's spring 2007 fashion show, the designer was at the bedside of her ailing father, who died that day. Despite her obvious loss, she carried through until the end of the show, when the appreciative applause of the fashionistas caused her to break down in tears.

For Dad: Wang cried as she accepted the applause and sympathy of the fashionistas at her show in September 2006. Her father had died earlier that day.

Sometimes Wang wonders what she will come up with next. "Sometimes I do worry, after a collection, 'Okay, what'll I do next?' But I've learned to relax a little, to give myself a break and trust that I will . . . find my inspiration."

Next Up?

What does Wang have in the works? She's already aced wedding invitations. Couples can choose an invitation style that suits them personally, from traditional and conservative to colorful and modern. "At best, invitations express a sense of originality and imagination," says Wang. "They speak to the unique personality of the bride and groom, and give the invited guests a wonderful, indelible first impression of the special celebration to come."

In 2007 she launched her Simply Vera line with Wisconsin-based Kohl's department stores. The ready-to-wear collection includes stylish but mid-priced clothing, lingerie, and accessories available in about one thousand stores nationwide. She also worked with Serta on the Vera Wang by Serta luxury beds. Her involvement included appearing in a commercial that says a bed should be, "luxurious, romantic, stylish, and comfortable." This effort ties into her desire "to go into more projects for the home, perhaps bed and bath items. We all care

With Kohl's: Wang and Kevin Mansell, president of Kohl's, Inc., pose together after the announcement that she would design clothing and accessories for the national department store.

about our homes and want to make them as comfortable as possible." In 2008 she launched a line of luxury linens. A new website called www.verawangonweddings.com will carry the bedding, as well as other Vera Wang products. "I'm a totally obsessive, passionate, mad woman," laughs Wang of her seemingly endless ideas and plans.

 Josephine and Cecilia have started to get involved in Mom's business. They have modeled her clothes and accessories from the Simply Vera line.

Vera Wang is very much her own woman. She has a unique way of seeing things, and she brings that vision to everything she creates. While success and selling clothes are important to Wang, staying true to her core is even more important. At the end of the day, Wang wants to make clothing that she likes.

Fortunately, with hard work—as well as with a few lucky breaks and the strong support of her family—Wang has been able to make clothes that she loves for many years. Looking ahead to the future, she hopes to keep doing so. After all, if there's one thing Vera Wang isn't very good at, it's standing still.

TIMELINE

mid-1940s   Cheng Ching Wang and his wife, Florence Wang, leave Shanghai, China, for the United States.

1949   Vera Wang is born on June 27.

1951   Kenneth Wang is born.

1957   Vera begins taking ballet lessons.

1959   Vera seriously takes up figure skating.

1950s-1960s   Vera attends the all-girls Chapin School in New York. She goes to fashion shows in Paris, France, with her mother.

1967   Vera begins to skate in pairs with James Stuart.

1968   Vera and James participate in the U.S. Figure Skating Championships with the hope of going to the 1968 Olympics. They do not qualify. Vera participates in the International Debutante Ball in New York. Vera enrolls at Sarah Lawrence College in its premed program.

1969   Vera and James come in fifth in the U.S. Figure Skating Championships. She decides to give up skating.

1970   Vera moves to Paris, where she has a brief romance with French figure skater Patrick Pera *(right)*. Vera reenters Sarah Lawrence, this time as an art history major.

1971   Vera graduates from Sarah Lawrence. *Vogue* magazine hires her as an assistant.

1972   *Vogue* promotes Wang to fashion editor, the youngest in the magazine's history.

1973   *Vogue* promotes Wang to senior fashion editor.

1980   Wang meets Arthur Becker for the first time at a tennis tournament.

1987   Wang leaves *Vogue* to work for Ralph Lauren as a design director. She starts dating Arthur Becker seriously. They become engaged.

1989   Wang grows frustrated as she searches for the perfect wedding dress. She marries Becker in a dress she designed. She leaves Ralph Lauren.

1990   Wang opens the Vera Wang Bridal House Ltd, which offers wedding gowns made by top-notch designers.

1991   Wang and Becker adopt a daughter named Cecilia.

1992–1994   Wang designs her own line of bridal gowns and evening wear to positive reviews. She creates a dazzling figure skating outfit for Olympic skater Nancy Kerrigan. Vera and Arthur adopt another daughter named Josephine.

1995   Sharon Stone and Holly Hunter wear Vera Wang gowns to the Academy Awards, bringing Wang further publicity.

1997   Wang designs the wedding dress for Karenna Gore *(below)*, daughter of Vice President Al Gore.

1998   Wang designs a dress for First Lady Hillary Rodham Clinton. Vera comes out with a bridal Barbie doll.

1999–2000   Wang's designs for celebrity weddings and awards cere-monies—including Posh Spice, Vanessa Williams, and Kristi Yamaguchi—bring her increased fame. Wang contracts with Unilever to create a signature perfume.

2001   Wang publishes *Vera Wang on Weddings*.

2002   Wang debuts her perfume, Vera Wang Eau de Parfum, to record sales.

2003   The perfume wins the FiFi award from the Fragrance Foundation for best perfume. Wang designs the outfits for the Philadelphia Eagles cheerleaders.

2004   Florence Wang dies.

2005   Chet Hazzard, Wang's longtime business partner, dies. Wang and her father visit Shanghai, China, together. She designs a lux-ury suite at the Halekulani Hotel *(below)* in Honolulu, Hawaii.

2006   Cheng Ching Wang dies.

2007   Wang launches her Simply Vera line with Wisconsin-based Kohl's department stores.

2008   Wang launches the Vera Wang by Serta luxury beds. She adds luxury linens that will be sold through a new e-commerce website, www.verawangonweddings.com. The Fragrance Foundation honors her with its Hall of Fame award.

GLOSSARY

Academy Awards (Oscars): a set of annual awards that honors the best motion pictures, performances, writing, and production of the previous year

Barbie doll: first launched in 1959, Barbie was the brainchild of Ruth and Elliot Handler. Ruth saw a svelte doll named Lilli in postwar Germany. She decided to create a purely U.S. version and named it after her daughter. Her son, Ken, was the name given to Barbie's boyfriend doll. The Handlers and their friend Harold Mattson founded Mattel (Matt and El). Barbie dolls have been following fashion trends—including the popularity of Vera Wang wedding dresses—ever since.

Bryant Park: located in midtown Manhattan, the park has many outdoor amenities. But for Vera Wang, the park has become the place where twice-yearly fashion shows are held in tents.

Chapin School: an all-girls school for children from kindergarten to twelfth grade in Manhattan

couture: a French word meaning "sewing" or "dressmaking." At the highest (haute) levels, haute couture means clothing of the finest kind, usually from designers in Italy, France, or the United States.

couture

Emmy Awards (Emmys): a set of annual awards that honors the best in television programming and performance

fashion design: an art form dedicated to the design of clothing and accessories created within the cultural and social influences of a specific era

fashionista: a person who avidly follows fashion trends, most often by working within the high-fashion industry

fashion show: an event that showcases the clothing of fashion designers

fertility treatment: medical procedures, including drugs, that are meant to help a couple conceive a child

Fragrance Foundation: set up in 1949, a nonprofit agency whose mission is to develop programs that educate people around the world about the importance and pleasures of fragrance. Wang won the FiFi, the foundation's highest award, in 2003. She was given the Hall of Fame award in 2008 for her ongoing contributions to the fragrance industry.

Golden Globe Awards: a set of annual awards chosen by the Hollywood Foreign Press Association. The awards recognize outstanding U.S. and foreign achievements in movies and television.

made-to-order clothing: unique designs that are made only for the one person who will wear them

Olympic Games: based on an ancient tradition, sporting contests that bring together the best athletes from around the world to compete in winter and summer sports

photo shoot: a session in which models or props are carefully set up, lit, and photographed for publication in magazines

ready-to-wear clothing: designs that are made in sizes that fit most people and that are marketed in a finished condition rather than needing special alterations

runway: the long, narrow, usually elevated platform that models walk on when they show off clothing at a fashion show

Sorbonne: historically, the name of part of the University of Paris system of colleges. The system has thirteen different universities, four of which include the name Sorbonne and have facilities

runway

in the historical building, called the Sorbonne, located in Paris's fifth arrondissement (administrative division).

Sorbonne

Martha Stewart: a television personality whose opinions and advice about home decor, crafts, style, and cooking have made her a household name

trunk show: a special sale, often used by small businesses, in which designers show new products directly to store buyers or select customers at a retail store or boutique. Buyers are thus able to preview and/or purchase merchandise before it is made available to the public. It is particularly desirable to have the actual designer present at the event. When Wang first started her business, she used trunk shows to get interest in her gowns from high-end department stores.

U.S. Figure Skating Championships: also called Nationals, the annual competition organized by the U.S. Figure Skating Association. Not only are medals awarded, but the winners form the U.S. teams that go to the World Figure Skating Championships and the Winter Olympics.

SOURCE NOTES

4 Lisa Coleman, "A Designing Woman," *Forbes*, April 26, 1993, 118.

5 Marylin Johnson, "The World of Vera Wang," *Atlanta Journal-Constitution*, March 4, 2004, http://ajc.com/living/content/living/fashion/0303/07wang.html (December 14, 2005).

7 Cynthia Sanz and Sue Miller, "Chic to Chic," *People*, July 20, 1998, 129.

11 Ibid.

11 Barbara Kantrowitz, Holly Peterson, and Pat Wingert, "How I Got There: Vera Wang," *Newsweek*, October 24, 2005, http://msnbc.msn.com/id/9756475/site/newsweek/ (August 16, 2006).

12 Nadia Mustafa, "Vera Wang," *Time Online Edition*, Fall 2005, http://www.time.com/time/2005/style/091305/vera_wang_56_designer_33a.html (August 16, 2006).

12 Shane Mitchell, "Wang's World," *Travel and Leisure*, October 2005, http://www.travelandleisure.com (December 14, 2005).

14 Sanz and Miller, "Chic to Chic," 129.

17 Kantrowitz, Peterson, and Wingert, "How I Got There."

21 Janet Carlson Freed, "Designer of Dreams," *Town & Country*, February 2002.

21 Ibid.

21 Sanz and Miller, "Chic to Chic," 129.

23 Kantrowitz, Peterson, and Wingert, "How I Got There."

23 Suzy Menkes, "Taking China: Vera Wang's Long March," *International Herald Tribune*, November 8, 2005, http://www.iht.com/articles/2005/11/07/style/fwang.php (December 20, 2005).

23 Sanz and Miller, "Chic to Chic," 129.

24 Kantrowitz, Peterson, and Wingert, "How I Got There."

24 Ibid.

25 Freed, "Designer of Dreams."

25 Amy Larocca, "Vera Wang's Second Honeymoon," *New York Magazine*, January 23, 2006, http://nymag.com/nymetro/news/people/features/15541/index.html (August 16, 2006).

26 Sanz and Miller, "Chic to Chic," 129.

27 Ibid.

27 Kantrowitz, Peterson, and Wingert, "How I Got There."

28   Larocca, "Vera Wang's Second Honeymoon."

29–30   Ibid.

30   Ibid.

31   Sanz and Miller, "Chic to Chic," 129.

31   Freed, "Designer of Dreams."

· 31   Vera Wang, *Vera Wang on Weddings*, New York: HarperResource, 2001, 14.

32   Ibid.

33   Sanz and Miller, "Chic to Chic," 129.

33–34   Jeffrey Zaslow, "Vera Wang," *USA Weekend*, May 8, 1997, http://www.usaweekend.com/98_issues/980510/980510talk_wang.html (August 16, 2006).

35   Sanz and Miller, "Chic to Chic," 129.

35   Larocca, "Vera Wang's Second Honeymoon."

35   Ibid.

36   Serena French, "Wang's World," *Flare*, February 2004.

37   Freed, "Designer of Dreams."

37   Menkes, "Taking China."

39   Freed, "Designer of Dreams."

39   Sanz and Miller, "Chic to Chic," 129.

39   Coleman, "A Designing Woman," 118.

39   Ibid.

40   Sanz and Miller, "Chic to Chic," 129.

42   *In Style*, "The Look of Vera Wang," February 2004.

43   French, "Wang's World."

43   Ibid.

44   Michelle Tauber and Rebecca Paley, "Wang's World," *People*, March 22, 2004, 107–108.

44   Freed, "Designer of Dreams."

45   Jane Sharp, "Vera Wang and Her Glamorous Gowns," *Biography*, June 1998, 60.

47   Hal Rubenstein, "The Look of Vera Wang," *In Style*, December 200, 142.

47   Ibid.

47   Melissa Ceria, "The Search for the Perfect Dress," *Town & Country*, August 2003.

47–48   Adena Halpern, "The Vera." *Marie Claire*, March 2005, 244.

48 Rubenstein, "The Look of Vera Wang," 142.

48 Ibid.

48 Ibid.

48 Samantha Critchell, "Vera Wang Is a Favorite with Celebrities," *Chicago Daily Southtown*, September 25, 2005, http://www.dailysouthtown.com/southtown/dsliving/2511dlgd.htm (December 14, 2005).

49 *Cosmopolitan*, "Movie-Star Mannequins," October 1998.

49 Rubenstein, "The Look of Vera Wang," 142.

50 Ibid.

50 Ibid.

50 *In Style*, "The Look of Vera Wang," February 2004, 84–88.

50 Ibid.

52 Johnson, "The World of Vera Wang."

53 Donna Bulseco, "Brides, Revisited," *In Style*, Spring 2002.

54 Ibid.

55 Ibid.

55 Ibid.

56 Sanz and Miller, "Chic to Chic," 129.

56 Ibid.

57 Ibid.

60 Bulseco, "Brides, Revisited."

60 Ibid.

62 Ibid.

62 Sanz and Miller, "Chic to Chic," 129.

62 *In Style*, "The Look of Vera Wang," February 2004.

64 Freed, "Designer of Dreams."

64 Clarissa Cruz, "Vera Firma," *Entertainment Weekly*, November 16, 2001.

64 French, "Wang's World."

64–65 Ibid.

65 Sanz and Miller, "Chic to Chic," 129.

66 Menkes, "Taking China."

67 Critchell, "Vera Wang Is a Favorite."

68 Freed, "Designer of Dreams."

68 Tauber and Paley, "Wang's World."

69 Sanz and Miller, "Chic to Chic," 129.

69   Tauber and Paley, "Wang's World."

69   Johnson, "The World of Vera Wang."

69   Tauber and Paley, "Wang's World."

69   Kantrowitz, Peterson, and Wingert, "How I Got There."

70   Ibid.

70   Freed, "Designer of Dreams."

70–71 Ibid.

71   Johnson, "The World of Vera Wang."

71   Freed, "Designer of Dreams."

73   Sharp, "Vera Wang and Her Glamorous Gowns."

73   Johnson, "The World of Vera Wang."

73   Kantrowitz, Peterson, and Wingert, "How I Got There."

73   Johnson, "The World of Vera Wang."

74   Mitchell, "Wang's World."

74   Ibid.

74   Stacie Stukin and Jeryl Brunner, "Shelf Absorbed," *In Style*, January 2001.

74   Freed, "Designer of Dreams."

74   *In Style*, "For the Bride: Vera Wang for Vera Wang," November 2004.

74   Hal Rubenstein, "Vera Unveiled," *In Style*, September 2002, 578.

75   Larocca, "Vera Wang's Second Honeymoon."

75   Sanz and Miller, "Chic to Chic," 129.

75   Critchell, "Vera Wang Is a Favorite."

78   Sanz and Miller, "Chic to Chic," 129.

79   Stukin and Brunner, "Shelf Absorbed."

79   Menkes, "Taking China."

79   Ibid.

79   Ibid.

79   Mustafa, "Vera Wang."

80   Tauber and Paley, "Wang's World."

80   Ibid.

80   Cruz, "Vera Firma."

80–81 Mitchell, "Wang's World."

82   Tauber and Paley, "Wang's World."

82   Freed, "Designer of Dreams."

82–83 Ibid.

83   *People*, "Ten Most Romantic Couples of 1995," February 13, 1995, 68.

83   Ibid.

83   Hal Rubenstein, "At Home with Vera Wang," *In Style*, December 2005.

84   Stukin and Brunner, "Shelf Absorbed."

84–85   *Toronto Star*, "Vera Wang Pass the Prozac," September 22, 2005, C06.

85–86   Kate Reardon, "Some Rare Finds Make Me Consider Selling a Kidney So I Can Afford Them," *Times*, November 5, 2005, http://web31 .epnet.com/citation (December 2, 2005).

86   Critchell, "Vera Wang Is a Favorite."

89   Freed, "Designer of Dreams."

89   Marnie Hayutin, "Fashionable Invitations," *Cincinnati*, January 2, 2006, http://web31epnet.com/Delivery/Print/Save.asp (January 15, 2006).

90   Serta Commercial starring Vera Wang, available online at http:// www.serta.com/vw/index.php (May 6, 2008).

90–91   Johnson, "The World of Vera Wang."

91   Tauber and Paley, "Wang's World."

SELECTED BIBLIOGRAPHY

Business Wire, "Vera Wang Boutique at Halekulani Opens: The First-Ever Vera Wang Lifestyle Boutique in the World," January 5, 2006, http://home.businesswire.com/portal/site/google/index.jsp?ndmViewId=news (January 14, 2006).

Coleman, Lisa. "A Designing Woman." *Forbes*, April 26, 1993, 118.

Critchell, Samantha. "Vera Wang Is a Favorite with Celebrities." *Chicago Daily Southtown*, September 25, 2005. http://www.dailysouthtown.com/southtown/dsliving/2511dlgd.htm (December 14, 2005).

Gerston, Jill. "Vera Wang." *Biography*, March 2001, 38.

Halpern, Adena. "The Vera." *Marie Claire*, March 2005, 244.

Johnson, Marylin. "The World of Vera Wang." *Atlanta Journal-Constitution*, March 4, 2004. http://ajc.com/living/content/living/fashion/0303/07wang.html (December 14, 2005).

Kantrowitz, Barbara, Holly Peterson, and Pat Wingert. "How I Got There: Vera Wang." *Newsweek*, October 24, 2005. http://msnbc.msn.com/id/9756475/site/newsweek/ (August 16, 2006).

Larocca, Amy. "Vera Wang's Second Honeymoon." *New York Magazine*, January 23, 2006. http://nymag.com/nymetro/news/people/features/15541/index.html (August 16, 2006).

Menkes, Suzy. "Taking China: Vera Wang's Long March." *International Herald Tribune*, November 8, 2005. http://www.iht.com/articles/2005/11/07/style/fwang.php (December 20, 2005).

Mitchell, Shane. "Wang's World." *Travel and Leisure*, October 2005. http://www.travelandleisure.com (December 14, 2005).

Mustafa, Nadia. "Vera Wang." *Time Online Edition*, Fall 2005. http://www.time.com/time/2005/style/091305/vera_wang_56__designer_33a.html (August 16, 2006).

Rath, Paula. "Vera Wang Breaks New Ground." *Honolulu Advertiser*, January 13, 2006.

Rubenstein, Hal. "The Look of Vera Wang." *In Style*, December 2000, 142.

——"Vera Unveiled." *In Style*, September 2002, 578.

Sanz, Cynthia, and Sue Miller. "Chic to Chic." *People*, July 20, 1998, 129.

Sharp, Jane. "Vera Wang and Her Glamorous Gowns." *Biography*, June 1998, 60.

Stukin, Stacie, and Jeryl Brunner. "Shelf Absorbed." *In Style*, January 2001.

Tauber, Michelle, and Rebecca Paley. "Wang's World." *People*, March 22, 2004, 107–108.

Toronto Star, "Vera Wang Is Tops." June 9, 2005. http://web31.epnet.com/citation.asp (December 12, 2005).

Zaslow, Jeffrey. "Vera Wang." *USA Weekend*, May 8, 1997. http://www.usaweekend.com/98_issues/980510/980510talk_wang.html (August 16, 2006).

FURTHER READING AND WEBSITES

Books

Behnke, Alison. *Chinese in America*. Minneapolis: Lerner Publications Company, 2005.

Bell, Alison. *Fearless Fashion*. Montreal: Lobster Press, 2004.

Gourley, Catherine. *Ms. and the Material Girls*. Minneapolis: Twenty-First Century Books, 2008.

Hartsog, Debbie. *Creative Careers in Fashion*. New York: Allworth Press, 2006.

Hill, Anne E. *Michelle Kwan*. Minneapolis: Twenty-First Century Books, 2004.

Koopersmith, Chase. *How to Be a Teen Fashionista*. Beverly, MA: Fair Winds Press, 2005.

McAlpine, Margaret. *Working in the Fashion Industry*. Milwaukee: Gareth Stevens Publishing, 2006.

Miller, Brandon Marie. *Dressed for the Occasion: What Americans Wore 1620–1970*. Minneapolis: Twenty-First Century Books, 1999.

Todd, Anne M. *Vera Wang*. New York: Chelsea House, 2007.

Wang, Vera. *Vera Wang on Weddings*. New York: HarperResource, 2001.

Websites

Fashionclub.com

http://www.fashionclub.com

This teen website offers advice on fashion and makeup, as well as career information.

Teen Vogue

http://www.teenvogue.com

This site, created for teens who are into fashion, offers tips on how to accessorize and design clothes, as well as background on modeling and fashion as a career.

Vera Wang

http://www.verawang.com

This site shows Vera Wang products of all kinds, from dresses to eyeglasses.

PHOTO ACKNOWLEDGMENTS

The images in this book are used with the permission of: © Jemal Countess/WireImage/ Getty Images, p. 1; © Getty Images, p. 3; © iStockphoto.com/Glenn Bo, p. 4; Charles Sykes/Rex Features USA, p. 5; © Mitchell Gerber/CORBIS, pp. 6 (right), 23; © Slim Aarons/Hulton Archive/Getty Images, p. 8; © Topical Press Agency/Hulton Archive/ Getty Images, pp. 9, 10 (top); © Laura Westlund/Independent Picture Service, p. 10 (bottom); © John Chillingworth/Hulton Archive/Getty Images, p. 11; Seth Poppel Yearbook Library, p. 12; AP Photo, p. 13; © AFP/Getty Images, pp. 15, 92; © L. V. Clark/ Fox Photos/Hulton Archive/Getty Images, pp. 16, 98; © David Gould/Globe Photos, Inc., p. 18; © Reg Lancaster/Hulton Archive/Getty Images, p. 19; © Ron Galella/WireImage/ Getty Images, p. 21; Francesco Scavullo/*VOGUE* Magazine Copyright © 1974 Condé Nast Publications Inc., p. 22; © Andrea Blanch/Hulton Archive/Getty Images, p. 24; © Barry King/WireImage/Getty Images, p. 25; © Tom Gates/Hulton Archive/Getty Images, p. 26; © David Lees/CORBIS, p. 28; © Jack Robinson/Hulton Archive/Getty Images, p. 30; © Pacific Stock/SuperStock, p. 32; © Mirrorpix/Everett Collection, p. 33; © Lynn Goldsmith/CORBIS, pp. 34, 52; © Judie Burstein/Globe Photos, Inc., p. 36; © Barron Claiborne/CORBIS, p. 38; © Rafael Fuchs/CORBIS, p. 40; © Matthew Peyton/ Getty Images, p. 42; © Deborah Feingold/CORBIS, p. 43; AP Photo/Louis Lanzano, p. 46; © Robin Platzer/Twin Images/Time & Life Pictures/Getty Images, p. 48; Stewart Cook/ Rex Features USA, p. 49 (left); © Mike Powell/Allsport/Getty Images, p. 51 (bottom); © Callie Shell/White House/Time & Life Pictures/Getty Images, pp. 54, 93; © Luke Frazza/AFP/Getty Images, p. 55; AP Photo/Jim Cooper, p. 58; © Konrad Zelazowski/ Alamy, p. 60; © Barry Talesnick/Retna Ltd., p. 61; © Timothy A. Clary/AFP/Getty Images, p. 63 (bottom); © Dimitrios Kambouris/Fashion Wire Daily/Retna Ltd., p. 64; © Andrea Renault/Globe Photos, Inc., p. 66; AP Photo/Richard Drew, pp. 68, 88 (bottom left), 89; © Frazer Harrison/Getty Images, p. 70; © Rob Loud/Getty Images, p. 71; © Joe Robbins/ Getty Images, p. 72 (bottom); © Rabbani and Solimene Photography/WireImage/Getty Images, pp. 75 (left), 82; © Francois Guillot/AFP/Getty Images, p. 75 (right); © Jennifer Graylock/Retna Ltd., p. 76; © Liu Jin/AFP/Getty Images, p. 78; © Business Wire/Getty Images, pp. 81, 94; © Mark Mainz/Getty Images, pp. 85 (both), 86 (both); AP Photo/ Jennifer Graylock, p. 88 (top left); Rex Features USA, p. 88 (top and bottom right); © LRRB and Co./WireImage/Getty Images, p. 90.

Front Cover: © Evan Agostini/Getty Images.

ABOUT THE AUTHOR

Katherine Krohn is the author of many books for young readers, including *Ella Fitzgerald: First Lady of Song, Rosie O'Donnell, Princess Diana, Shakira, Gwen Stefani*, and *Wild West Women*. Krohn is also a fiction writer and an artist. She lives with her family in Oregon.